THE
EDWARDIAN
LADY

Frontispiece: *The artist Edith Holden at her easel*
(By permission of Mrs Anne Williams)

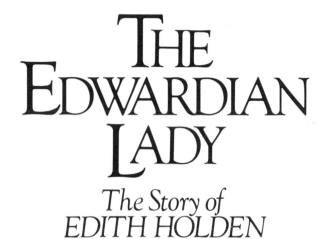

THE EDWARDIAN LADY

The Story of
EDITH HOLDEN

Author of
The Country Diary of an Edwardian Lady

Compiled by
INA TAYLOR

Holt, Rinehart and Winston
New York

First published in the United States in 1980 by
Holt, Rinehart and Winston, 383 Madison Avenue,
New York, New York 10017.

Library of Congress Cataloging in Publication Data

Taylor, Ina.
    The Edwardian Lady.

    "A Webb & Bower Book."
    Bibliography: p. 202
    1. Holden, Edith, 1871-1920. 2.Naturalist—
England—Biography. 3. Illustrators—England—
Biography. I. Title.
QH31.H65T39 1980   574'.092'4 [B]   80-12677
ISBN 0–03 057454–4

A *Webb & Bower* BOOK
Webb & Bower Ltd., Exeter, England
Printed in Italy by Arnoldo Mondadori Editore

10 9 8 7 6 5 4 3 2

CONTENTS

INTRODUCTION

It is ironic that Edith Holden's fame rests not on the several books she illustrated in her lifetime, nor on the fifty or so oil paintings she exhibited, but on a private note-book she never intended to publish.

There is in fact nothing unusual about Edith's diary. Many Victorian and Edwardian ladies kept journals, and most middle-class young ladies learned to sketch flowers and landscapes, and paint them in watercolours. To combine the journal and the sketching was not a new idea either, and young ladies frequently illustrated entries about their holidays with suitable little landscapes in watercolours. At school, girls were encouraged to observe the changing seasons and illustrate them in conjunction with apt quotations from literature, and several were produced for 1906 with a marked similarity to Edith Holden's *Nature Notes*, which were published in 1977 under the title *The Country Diary of an Edwardian Lady*. Although it could never have been published at the time it was written, this journal became an immediate best-seller seventy years later. We are now very conscious of our vanishing countryside and this, combined with a nostalgia for the turn of the century, ensured that this delicately executed piece of work would gain international popularity. It portrays a deep appreciation of nature which is like a balm to us in our noisy, fast-moving world.

Although Edith's *Nature Notes* were by no means unusual, it must also be said that her family and her life did differ from most middle-class families at the end of the nineteenth century. In the book she gives only a few

6

tantalizing references to herself and her family such as: "My sister brought home some beautiful White Meadow Saxifrage she had picked in some fields near Hatton," or more elusive comments: "G. brought in some blossoms of the Dusky Cranesbill today," and "Miss F. gave me some Bee Orchids this afternoon." It is fascinating to read about her weekly ride to Knowle without ever learning the reason for it.

We look at a whole year through Edith's eyes, kneel down and peer among the primrose leaves for signs of buds, and yet when we get to the end of December we know very little about the person whose eyes we have been borrowing.

Edith's writing is very clear and direct, without either the studied literary style or the sentimentality one expects in lady diarists of that period. She writes as a naturalist making an objective record. Seeing the dusky cranesbill she comments: "In all probability the seed of the plant had been carried there from some garden, as this plant is very rare in its wild state." There are no effusive adjectives to ward off the modern reader, and much of the book's charm lies in the fact that it is a working note-book for the naturalist and at the same time for the artist. Edith notes briefly the detail necessary for her painting: the parasol fungus is simply "pale fawn, flecked and shaded with darker tones of the same colour", and the wild-service has "the upper part of the foliage crimson and scarlet and the lower deep orange". Throughout we are aware of a practical individual who can get on without a fuss whether it be to plunge through nettles to find the wild canterbury bell or to carry her bicycle over a muddy patch.

From her writing we get the idea of a quiet observer, a gentle person who can gain simple amusement from "one precocious young robin trying to capture a worm, nearly three times as long as itself'', and those who met her remembered her for her gentleness and affection.

Edith came from a very talented family, and her sisters gained greater recognition in their lifetime for their literary and artistic works than she did for hers. By the time of her marriage, however, when she was nearly forty, she had established herself as a book illustrator and she continued working until her tragic death in 1920. Throughout her life she had followed the tradition of her Victorian predecessors, ladies of widely varying ability, who filled their days with music, painting and poetry. Her work is evidence of an exceptional talent and sensitivity, in which she was encouraged from an early age by her family and the surroundings of her youth.

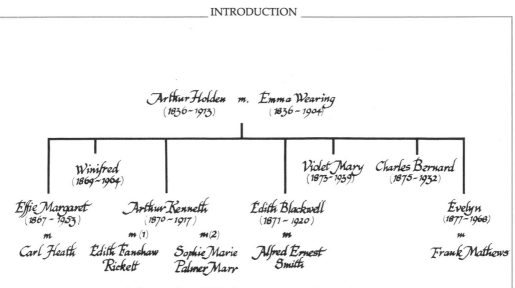

A chart to show Edith, her parents, brothers and sisters.

CHAPTER
ONE

HOLLY GREEN, MOSELEY

1871 to 1880

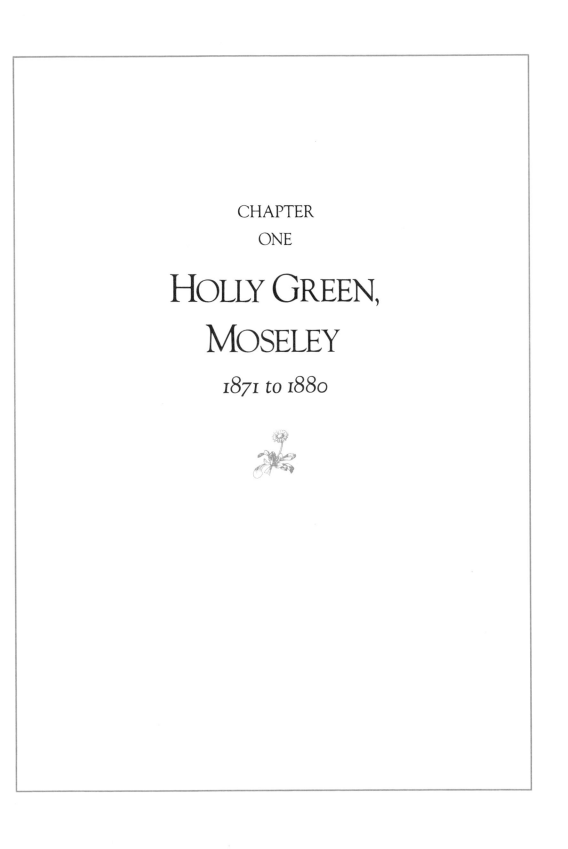

In 1865 an ambitious young man of thirty left his home town of Bristol after the death of his father, and with a small inheritance set out for Birmingham.

In the later nineteenth century this fast-growing new industrial centre was an exciting place — if you were one of the fortunate minority living above subsistence level. For men of initiative Birmingham offered seemingly limitless opportunities. As a product of the Industrial Revolution it had grown rapidly to become one of the country's leading manufacturing towns, where coal mines and iron foundries provided materials for many products from railway carriages to buttons. Since Birmingham was very much a "new" town it was free from the grip of the guilds and their rigid apprenticeships; success was open to anyone, irrespective of background, who had energy, foresight and capital.

On his arrival the young man, Arthur Holden, found a partner and bought out a firm of varnish-makers called Jeremiah Barrett and Company, who were having financial difficulties following some unprofitable speculation in American turpentine. Within three years he was in sole control of the firm, and the partner, a Mr Sanders, had faded into the background.

Holden came from a Nonconformist family, and like them held strongly to the Unitarian church. Earlier in the nineteenth century there were strict laws against Nonconformists and because the universities closed their doors to such dissenters many able men turned their talents directly to industry. Legislation had also forbidden Nonconformist clergymen to live within five miles of a corporate town, but Birmingham, not having achieved that status, was a natural haven for dissenters. They came and they flourished. It is no accident that many nationally known firms such as Cadbury and Taylor & Lloyds, which later became Lloyds Bank, both of which were founded by Quaker families, have Nonconformist origins in Birmingham. The huge corporation of G.K.N. began life when the

Arthur Holden c. 1870;
the portrait is one of a collection showing the
Central Literary Association's
original members.

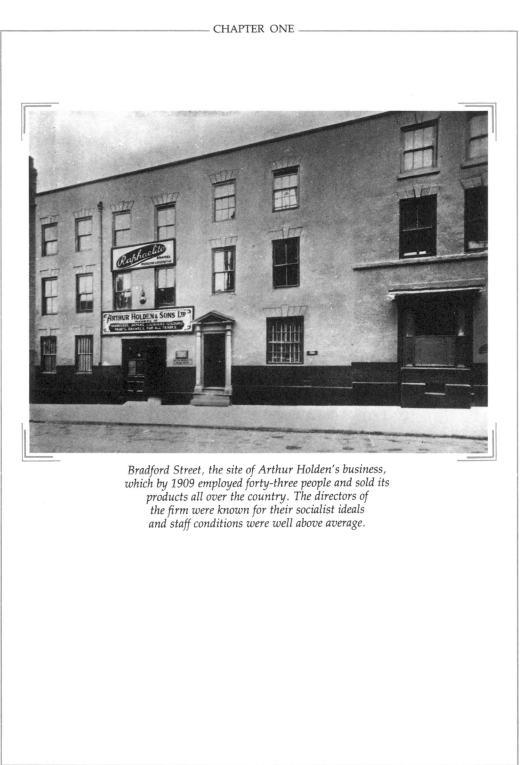

*Bradford Street, the site of Arthur Holden's business,
which by 1909 employed forty-three people and sold its
products all over the country. The directors of
the firm were known for their socialist ideals
and staff conditions were well above average.*

A photograph taken about 1895, on one of their outings,
of some of the poor children from the Birmingham
slums, whom the Holdens and others tried
to help. The boys and the girls went on
separate outings.

Unitarian Joseph Chamberlain came to Birmingham in 1854. Arthur Holden was therefore able to see a future here for someone of his persuasion. He also found the political climate of the town highly congenial since his views were Liberal, even Radical, very much in accord with those of the men who sat on the town council, and he was an admirer and supporter of the Radical John Bright who had stood for Parliament for Birmingham in the 1860s.

Very much a part of his strong religious and political convictions was a real desire to help the less fortunate, and the slums of Birmingham produced many of these. For them, the town was far from being the centre of free enterprise and prosperity; theirs was a grim, hard-working existence in unsavoury surroundings, a constant struggle against disease and the threat of the work-house. Philanthropy was fashionable: the men sent donations from their businesses and their wives made blankets or sent parcels of clothing for poor children, as did Arthur Holden, whose religion was essentially inspired by socialism. In many cases this charity did spring from a genuine wish to help.

Holden had a great personal interest in the arts. He was a well-read man who would have found Birmingham a more stimulating environment than might be imagined. Factory owners in many instances were patrons who were keen to spread an appreciation of the arts and music to all classes. Successive town councils pursued the policy of providing free cultural facilities and a central lending library. In art particularly the town was well served with galleries at the Royal Birmingham Society of Artists, where the two exhibitions every year attracted great interest. A museum was established, and there was also the Municipal Art School, which had a reputation for being the best art school outside London. In the middle of the century the first performance of Mendelssohn's oratorio *Elijah* took place in Birmingham, which gives an indication of the status the town had achieved.

Just before leaving Bristol, Arthur Holden had married a governess called Emma Wearing, a well-educated woman of his own age. With Elizabeth Bennett, a young servant aged twelve, they went to Aston, a village to the north of Birmingham. As the family began to grow and the business to establish itself, they moved house on several occasions, and by the time their daughter Edith was born they were living in a house called Holly Green in Church Road, Moseley.

Moseley was a village about two miles south of Birmingham. It was gradually expanding from a small rural community into a place for those who could afford to work in the town but live in the more congenial surroundings of the countryside. Church Road was mainly a new

Moseley village,
then in the parish of King's Norton, where Edith was born.
The photograph was taken in 1892 and in it can be seen
the church, the forge, the inn and
a florist and seedsman.

development behind the church and the older part of the village, where those who had made money in industry, such as the Holdens' neighbours, the Herberts, whose fortunes rested on the button industry, could rent suitable houses. The horse-trams and the railway station provided Arthur Holden with convenient transport to his firm in Bradford Street, near the centre of the town.

Edith was the fourth child in the Holdens' growing family. The eldest was Effie Margaret who was four years older and the second child was another daughter, Winifred, who had been born with a slight back deformity. Soon after the family's arrival at Holly Green, Arthur Holden was delighted with the birth of a son, Arthur Kenneth, and within a year after his birth Edith was born on 26th September 1871 and was given the second name of Blackwell, after a famous relative, better known in America than in England.

Elizabeth Blackwell, a cousin of the Holdens, was the first woman ever to qualify as a doctor, and on one of her lecture tours in England she met and inspired Elizabeth Garrett Anderson to follow suit. Elizabeth Blackwell's sister-in-law Lucy Stone was an ardent suffragette in America and so interested was Effie Holden in this that years later she wrote a short biography of her.

As the family grew Mrs Holden took on a local girl as nursemaid to the children. Rosamiah Gazey came to live with the family, sharing rooms at the top of the house with the maid, Elizabeth. Rosanna, as the children called her, was a very capable girl whom they grew to love, and long after the family had grown up she remained with them as "the old nanny". In the meantime she was kept very busy as more children arrived: after Edith came Violet Mary and then a second son, Charles Bernard, who like his brother was always known by his second name.

After the birth of the sixth child the family moved to a larger house called The Elms in another village, Acocks Green, a few miles south of Birmingham. Edith was then

five and able to remember this house later. Not long after the move, Mrs Holden had another daughter, Evelyn, who was to be the last in the family. Mrs Holden had delicate health and the seven pregnancies so close together had made her very weak. She never seemed to recover her strength fully and had to rest frequently. The baby Evelyn was also very frail and no one thought she would survive. More servants were taken on and Rosanna devoted herself to nursing the new baby.

The education of the children was very much in the hands of their mother. With her experience as a governess she set about teaching the older ones to read and write, and along with the formal exercises of the three "Rs", she taught them to appreciate literature from an early age. No child was too young to sit down and listen to her reciting a favourite poem. Those who were old enough memorized passages and proudly demonstrated their knowledge to their father later in the day. There were always lots of books in the house, particularly poetry, since Arthur Holden and his wife shared this interest.

Another pursuit which the children shared with their parents was walking in the country around Acocks Green. Arthur Holden loved the countryside and had a good knowledge of the birds and wild plants of the area. Mrs Holden was not always strong enough to accompany them, so the children made a special point of picking a colourful bunch of flowers to cheer her. Flowers were her special delight, both cultivated and wild, and she had a great appreciation of her garden. Her interest inspired the girls who also looked with great eagerness for the first aconite or the early buds on the honeysuckle. Even though a gardener was employed part-time his concern was more with producing vegetables.

During the time the children were young, Arthur Holden was very active in the public life of Birmingham. His paint and varnish firm settled down to steady production, his work-force grew and there were always plenty of people seeking the few vacancies that arose. He was very tolerant of genuine mistakes, never harsh and oppressive, and treated his workers with respect. Frederick Barlow, who worked at Arthur Holden & Sons for ten years from 1909 remembered Holden as "a sprightly old gentleman with snow white hair who used to come from Olton on the G.W.R. to Bordesley Station. He seemed very active for his age. I don't know how old he was, but all adults seem old to a boy of 13."

He has pleasant memories of the firm: "There was a family atmosphere about the firm, and it was generally understood that we must ALL work for the good of the firm, and most employees responded loyally." . . . "At the start of the [First World] War a lot of firms panicked and sacked their employees or put them on short time and reduced their wages, but not Holdens."

When Edith was only two, her father was elected to the Town Council, a great honour for someone newly arrived in the town.

This report in *The Birmingham Morning News* of 26th April 1873, part of a daily article giving short profiles of "Our Representatives" on the recently elected Town Council, shows the respect in which he was held. After explaining how he was elected, without opposition, to the ward of Deritend it went on: "He is a modest but able and intelligent councillor possessing literary ability of no mean order, and although not distinguished as an orator he finds an excellent field of labour on the Free Libraries Committee of which as well as the Baths and Parks he is a member."

Arthur Holden's period of service on the Town Council must have been an interesting one; he was working with Joseph Chamberlain during his third term of office as

Arthur Holden in later life. Arthur Matthison, who worked for him, said, "I thought him one of the finest elderly gentlemen I had ever met."

Mayor of Birmingham. Chamberlain's periods in office saw great improvements in the life of the town. Plans were made and carried out to make the water and gas supplies public utilities, and small committees were set up to investigate the best methods of carrying this out. Joseph Chamberlain and Arthur Holden were members of the Gas Committee during this time.

Besides his contact with Chamberlain on the Council, Arthur Holden knew him well through the church as they were both Unitarians and worshipped at the Birmingham Labour Church. They were also both Liberals and for a time at least Holden was a member of the Liberal Party, to which Chamberlain belonged, but this was not a membership he actively kept up. Holden was also a very active member of the Central Literary Association, joining within a couple of years of moving to Birmingham and remaining a member all his life. The association met to debate philosophical and topical issues, to listen to recitals and recitations and to follow other learned and artistic pursuits. Arthur Holden frequently led debates and at various times served as secretary, president and editor of the magazine.

Thus in several areas he participated fully in the life of his adopted town, benefiting as much from the ideas of others as they did from his. As the children grew up they were very aware of the life of the town and went along with their mother to watch special events, such as the visit of Queen Victoria, and of the politician John Bright for the unveiling of a statue of him commemorating his contribution to public life.

Against this background it was not surprising that the children, especially the girls, had a better general knowledge and awareness than most of their contemporaries.

CHAPTER
TWO

TROUTBECK,
DARLEY GREEN

1880 to 1890

The smithy at Packwood, a busy place in the farming community.
The smith lived alongside his workshop. The village was
small, with only a school, the smithy,
a wheelwright's shop and a few cottages
for the farm workers.

With the ever-increasing demands of public life Arthur Holden came to appreciate more and more the rural quiet of his domestic life. As Birmingham continued to expand, the area around The Elms became more built up. Traffic on the main Warwick to Birmingham road had increased noticeably in the five years they had been there, so in 1880 the Holdens retreated further into the country, to Darley Green, a small hamlet in Packwood, some fifteen miles south of Birmingham.

They moved into Troutbeck, one of a pair of imposing semi-detached houses which had recently been built, with long gardens going down to a small stream, a tributary of the Cuttle Brook. It was ideal for the family. Mrs Holden

Packwood House in 1891,
a short walk from Troutbeck where the Holdens lived.
Both the house and grounds were extensive,
and must have been fascinating for
children to explore.

derived great enjoyment from the garden where she rested when she was ill. The move must also have been pleasant for the children who now had trees to climb and their own stream to play in.

At the side and back of their house were fields where sheep and cows grazed. Near the end of the garden ran the railway, providing the much needed link between Arthur Holden and his daily business.

The area could not have been a greater contrast to the one they had left. Packwood was made up of several small farms and Darley Green itself had only the new semi-detached houses, one cottage, and an old mill with a mill pond. The village of Packwood was larger. There was a blacksmith, a shop, a school and a few cottages belonging to the farms.

The village was very much under the influence of Packwood House, owned by the Oakes family. The children became well acquainted with the grounds and to a certain extent with the family. It was only a short walk from Troutbeck to the park and the girls often went through it with their mother, past the house with its impressive architecture. In the grounds were sundials and an elaborate topiary where the Sermon on the Mount was represented by large carefully trimmed yew trees, Jesus being the largest, the disciples next in size and an assortment of lesser trees standing for the multitude.

The fish-pond at Packwood House was a favourite of Edith's and many years later when she wrote her *Nature Notes* she went back to the pond in July, and on her weekly ride to Knowle she noted, "Had a beautiful white Water Lily given me from the pool at Packwood House."

The many farms in the area were an attraction for the children, and Edith particularly liked to see the newly born animals. Under the railway bridge and along the lane brought them to Poplar Farm, or if they followed the stream at the bottom of the garden across the meadows they came to the church and Packwood Hall. Although on

A photograph of one of the lovely country lanes around Packwood House,
taken in June 1892, where, as a girl, Edith used to walk
with her family. She also mentions the area frequently
in the Nature Notes.

The west front of Packwood Hall in 1891.
Edith loved to visit the place both as a child and later.
She says in the Nature Notes, *"In the garden of Packwood Hall*
adjoining the churchyard the borders were full of
large clumps of single snowdrops; I brought away a
great bunch."

a much smaller scale than Packwood House, the Hall had a romantic mediaeval charm.

Edith often visited the house and adjoining farm after her family left the area. In her *Nature Notes* she describes how on 24th February she "cycled to Packwood through Solihull and Bentley Heath" and "...in the garden of Packwood Hall adjoining the church-yard the borders were full of large clumps of single snow-drops. I brought away a great bunch. The farmer living there brought out a little lamb to show me, one of a family of three born that morning. I held it in my arms and it seemed quite fearless — poking its little black head up into my face." The farmer was then Edward Tallis who had taken over since their days at Troutbeck, but Edith's constant visits to the area kept her in touch.

In the meantime, lessons went on for the children. Mrs Holden continued with her daughters' education and the two sons, whom Arthur Holden was preparing to come into the business, went to school. Mrs Holden was widely read in the classics from Chaucer through to the most modern romantic poets like Bliss Carmen and Jean Ingelow. Literature was no drudgery for the girls; their mother's knowledge and enthusiasm was infectious and literature was something they all took to willingly and remained an interest all their lives.

There were times when Mrs Holden was ill for several weeks on end, and the running of the household fell very much to the older girls. Winnie in particular was practical and capable. Though quite small and frailer than the others she was well able to manage. It was a great relief to Arthur Holden to see the home so smoothly organized in spite of the difficult times. Winnie also took over the education of the two younger girls, Violet and Evelyn, carrying on where her mother had left off with lessons in history, French and German grammar, music and sketching.

When an aunt suggested that one or two of the girls might go and stay with her to relieve the burden on the house, it was Effie who accepted the offer and left for Bristol. Edith was now thirteen, and was about to enter the Birmingham School of Art. She had shown talent in sketching and had pressed her parents hard to let her go to the School of Art for proper lessons. She started in the Elementary class on Monday, Wednesday and Friday mornings. It was a requirement of the school that students had to pass the examination of the Department of Science and Art in freehand and model drawing within two years of entering the school or they would lose their place. This proved no problem and in the examinations the following April Edith B. Holden appears on the prize list as passing with an Excellent (the highest grade) in freehand. The prospectus of the school stated that those who were classed as Excellent receive ''prizes consisting of books, drawing and mathematical instruments, colours or crayons as they may select''. Her first year had been successful and enjoyable. One particular highlight of the year had been the visit of Edward Burne-Jones to the school. Burne-Jones was then President of the Royal Birmingham Society of Artists and had come to stay for a few days in his home town. The Art Gallery put on a special exhibition of his and George Watts's work which was well attended by the townspeople and certainly by the Holdens. Burne-Jones declined to lecture though he accepted an invitation to inspect the work at the Art School. This he did during Edith's geometry class.

*The Birmingham Art School, a corridor on the ground floor,
drawn by W. H. Cooper. It was one of the most important
art schools outside London and Edith, Evelyn and Violet all
studied there.*

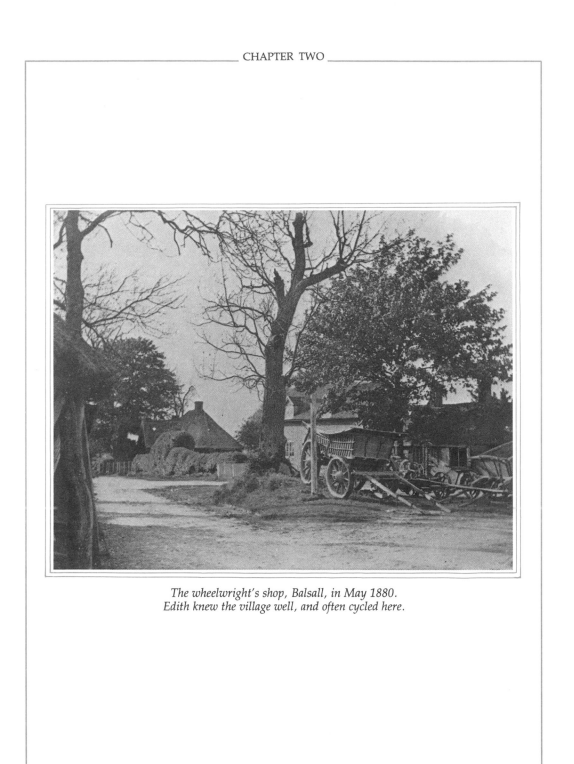

The wheelwright's shop, Balsall, in May 1880.
Edith knew the village well, and often cycled here.

Arthur Holden did not find it easy to keep up his public life from Darley Green. The distance from Birmingham made evening meetings difficult to attend in the winter and concern over his wife's health kept him more at home.

During her illness, Mrs Holden found her religion a great comfort. Like her husband she was a Unitarian. She had studied the Scriptures well and in her younger days published two little religious books for the Society for Promoting Christian Knowledge, entitled *Ursula's Girlhood* and *Beatrice of St. Mawse*. Over the years both husband and wife had also come to believe strongly in the spiritual world, and Mrs Holden believed that she had psychic powers and that on occasions she had received messages from "the other side".

In a philosophical essay which he wrote for the *Central Literary Magazine* on the subject of "Thoughts", Arthur Holden said that "occasionally and under special circumstances, a thought can be so strongly winged by the human will, that it can be made to find lodgment in the mind of another, with whom they are in affinity, irrespective of distance". He goes on in this article to suggest that the mind of a so-called genius is in fact often one which is more than most receptive to transmitted thought. To substantiate his point he reminds his readers "that Coleridge wrote the poem entitled *Kubla Khan* without, as he tells us, bringing into play his own mental faculties of composition, but merely recording the words as they came into his mind; an experience much less rare than is generally supposed". This last point he believed was borne out as Mrs Holden involved herself in automatic writing. At certain times she would take up a pen and write for a long time without any apparent knowledge of the content of her writing until the moment passed and she read the "alien" handwriting.

The whole family attended the Birmingham Labour Church in Hurst Street. They usually went to the Sunday evening service which had various socialist speakers. The girls found opportunities to help in the many philanthro-pic causes the Church sponsored, and they would gather flowers from the garden at Troutbeck, binding them with wool into little bunches to be taken by members of the Church to sick and poor children.

They had been very happy in the country but the distance from the railway station finally made journeys to Birmingham too complicated. In 1890, when Violet and Evelyn were old enough they wanted to join Edith at the Municipal School and Kenneth, the elder son, who had finished his elementary schooling, was taken into the family business, so in order to make the daily journey into Birmingham easier the family moved to an ideal house near Kingswood station — Gowan Bank.

CHAPTER
THREE

GOWAN BANK, KINGSWOOD

1890 to 1897

Gowan Bank was an old house in Kingswood, much larger and with more extensive gardens than Troutbeck. There was a small staff cottage nearby, and at the side of the house various out-buildings for the ponies and traps. Altogether it was a very impressive country residence, most suitable for the owner of a growing business.

Kingswood was another small village some sixteen miles out of Birmingham, but it had a distinct advantage over Darley Green in that the station was barely three hundred yards from the house. Gowan Bank and Kingswood Station were virtually the only two buildings in Station Road, the main part of the village being a little way further on. The railway line ran along the edge of their garden but this time in a cutting so hiding the railway.

The time at Gowan Bank was a very happy one for the family. The children were all beginning to branch out successfully in various fields, which was a great source of pleasure to their parents. The firm prospered without making undue demands on Arthur Holden, which enabled him to spend more time away from business concerns. Mrs Holden, although far from well, seemed able to take life gently and quietly at home. Some of the happiest family memories were of this house, so that when they moved to new houses later, the name was perpetuated.

Just after their arrival at Kingswood, Edith, then nineteen, was delighted by the acceptance of one of her pictures for the Royal Birmingham Society of Artists' Autumn Exhibition. The family attended the private viewing, since Arthur Holden was a subscriber to the Society, and were greatly delighted to see Edith's oil painting, *A Cosy Quartette*, hung along with the others.

Edith did well at the Municipal School that year, gaining an Excellent in her 3rd Grade examination in line drawing, and in her 2nd Grade Elementary modelling she gained a first-class grade. The examiner that year was Walter Crane.

She enjoyed her work at the Municipal School and was among stimulating company. At various times her fellow pupils included A. J. Gaskin, Sidney Meteyard, Charles Gere, Florence Rudland and Winifred Smith, all of whom became well-known book illustrators by the turn of the century.

The school enjoyed a good reputation as the best provincial art school, and was the first one allowed to hold the Examinations of the Department of Science and Art on its own premises instead of dispatching the students and their work by train to London.

In the National Competition a high percentage of the awards was gained by pupils from Birmingham. *The Studio* magazine, then in its infancy, published a long and glowing article on the work produced there.

As Edith completed her basic training, so Violet came to begin hers, and for a year they attended the school together. Edith was then ready to specialize, and animal painting seemed an obvious choice to her. She was fascinated by all wild life, both plant and animal, and loved to explore the countryside to find her models in their natural surroundings.

When she was twenty her tutors at the Municipal School suggested that it would be worth her while to study with Joseph Denovan Adam in Scotland. Denovan Adam was a painter who had recently set up a studio at his house, Craigmill, just outside Stirling, and who was rapidly gaining a reputation as a teacher of animal painting. He was himself a working artist, a member of a community of artists who had settled around Stirling and Cambuskenneth, a small village close by. The peaceful riverbanks, the beautiful old cottages, and the ancient castle and abbey attracted artists, some of whom came to work in the area for the summer, while others settled there permanently. The art school at Craigmill became a meeting place for local artists, visiting artists and students.

A contemporary of Denovan Adam described this rather special art school: "At Craigmill are paddocks and byres, stables and fields, in which cattle and sheep, horses and donkeys, fowls and geese are encouraged to think that life, after all, is well worth living. In comfortable stalls and loose boxes, or wandering untrammelled through the fresh green grass, they give in their varying moods and shifting attitudes, 'ample room and verge enough' to the painter's eye and hand. Here Denovan Adam, carries on the work he began more than thirty years ago among the Highland moors and rough hillside. He has gathered around him a knot of enthusiastic students, who have already given evidence that his thoroughly natural method of instruction is bound to produce good results."

From both the academic and domestic aspects there was much to recommend the school, and Mrs Holden was quite happy for Edith to be a residential student. Denovan Adam took as many as twenty-five students, most of whom were lodged locally, but a small number were accommodated in the house with his wife and children.

So in August 1891 Edith said farewell to her family. Although she was looking forward to the Scottish visit, it was the first time she had been away from home for so long. Her father travelled with her on the train from Birmingham to Carlisle, and on the next day to Edinburgh and eventually Stirling.

Edith was delighted by what she saw when they came into Stirling, the castle caught her eye immediately as it looked out over the town from its high rock. She could also see the famous Wallace Monument, on the other hill, towering over the wooded slopes of Abbey Craig, with Craigmill House at the foot. The setting could not have been better.

The pony and trap drove them from the station, along the River Forth and the edge of the dark coniferous woods of Abbey Craig to the gothic turret of Craigmill House where they were made welcome by the Adam family and the other students, so that when her father came to leave after a few days, Edith, although sad to see him go, was quite happy to remain. She settled in easily, soon becoming a great favourite with the children and well liked by the painter and his wife.

*Evelyn Holden in the garden at Gowan Bank, Kingswood, in
the 1890s. She would have been in her teens at this
time. She is painting a poster for one of
their charity events.*

*Arthur Holden at Kingswood in the 1890s. He was in his late
fifties at this time. Like his wife, he took great pleasure in
their garden.*

Life is like an April day,
All smiles and tears.
Happy they on Peace intent
Who can pluck the flower Content,
From its hopes and fears.

Through the storm and through the calm
Cometh Night apace,
Were the blossom sweetest yet,
When the golden Sun has set,
Who shall see its grace?

Yet though darkness hide the sky,
All is bright above.
Be it gloomy, be it fair, —
Cometh joy, or cometh care, —
God remaineth Love.

Aschesté

With sincerest good wishes.
Nov. 2. 1888.

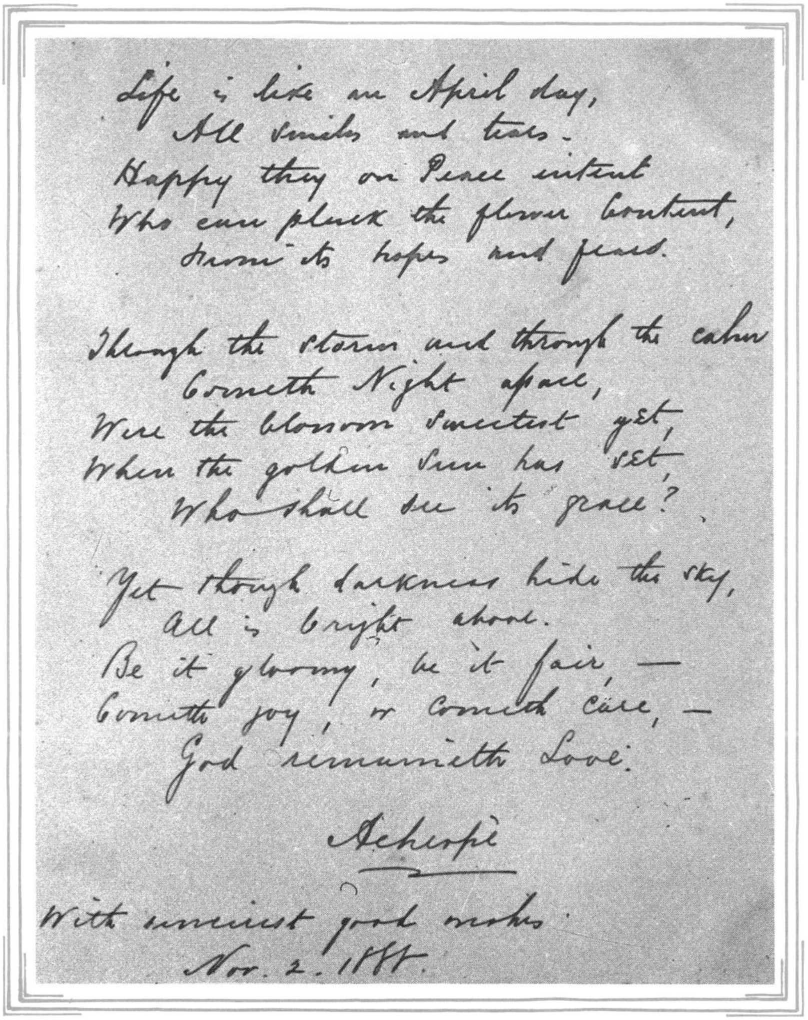

A poem composed by one of Arthur Holden's close friends in the Central Literary Association, Birmingham. He used the pseudonym Aschesté, and the poem is dated 2 November 1888.

She was fascinated by the various animals roaming freely in the park, which the students were encouraged to study. Mr Adam was always at hand to advise, suggest and encourage. One particular animal was chosen each day to be painted and the herdsman would bring it into the field in front of the house. Here there was a special studio built with glass sides, so that the students could continue painting even in the rain.

A small herd of Highland cattle was the great attraction at Craigmill, since these animals were not usually kept as far south as Stirling. A contemporary wrote: "To Highland cattle Denovan Adam's heart turns with especial fondness. He has made them his particular study, and is an authority on breeds and stock. Surely with their shaggy heads and long horns, they are the most picturesque of all cattle, and tone admirably with the rugged hillsides and long extending moors where they do most congregate. Over all horned beasts, Mr Adam has almost a magnetic power, he knows no fear of them and will walk up with confidence to the most truculent looking bull ... 'Don't be afraid of them, and you are all right,' so says Mr Adam."

Denovan Adam's approach to animals taught Edith a great deal and she became quite fearless. She would enter the field with her painting equipment and quietly settle herself near the grazing animal without any display of timidity. Her work developed well in this ideal environment, and her tutor was pleased with her progress.

*A portrait of Joseph Denovan Adam, the painter, who was born in 1842.
He studied art in London but later returned to Scotland
to set up a studio specializing in animal painting.
This photograph was taken not long before his
death in 1896.*

A painting by J. Denovan Adam called Bochastle, the Pass Leny.
It is typical of the rest of his work, and comes
from a series of paintings he exhibited in March 1895.
It also appears as the December picture in his
book, The Months in Scotland.

She adored Scotland and her letters home were filled with details of visits to the castle, walks through the woods of Abbey Craig and even her climb up the 246 steps to the top of Wallace Monument. She sent picture postcards of the famous sights as well as pieces of heather, all of which thrilled her sisters.

In her letters Edith told her family of the progress of Mr Adam's son, also called Denovan. The boy had been ill for some time and Edith always paid special attention to him. She sat with him and told him stories, or brought home from her rambles objects which she thought would particularly interest him, but eventually Denovan had to go away to Glasgow to be nursed, which worried them all at Craigmill. While he was away Edith wrote cheerful little notes with humorous sketches for Mr Adam to take to his son when he visited him.

A year went by quickly and the following August Mr Holden travelled to Stirling to bring Edith home. It was a happy reunion with her father, but a difficult parting from the Adam family and the animals which Edith had come to love. The year had been most enjoyable for her and she continued to make regular annual visits to Scotland. She also maintained a correspondence with the Adam family for several years.

Edith's work was very much influenced by Adam and the other artists she met. Her exhibition pieces at the Royal Birmingham Society of Artists regularly included Scottish work with titles like *Springtime: near Stirling*, *Highland Calves* and *Beside the Forth*. While she was away in

Dear Mʳˢ Holden
                Thank you very
very much for the pencil
case you sent me.
Wishing you a very merry
Xmas. With love from Denovan

A card to Edith's mother from Denovan Adam's son, with a painting by him. Edith had befriended him when she stayed with the family in Scotland, and he had continued to correspond with the Holden family.

Scotland, her sister Effie was in Sweden studying the Arts and Crafts Movement there. Swedish handicrafts had an unbroken tradition that was perpetuated in the work of the country people. During her study in Sweden Effie met Carl Heath, who like herself was studying the handicrafts with the intention of becoming a teacher. They became good friends and kept in contact after her return, and eventually in 1900, after a trip round the world and a stay in New Zealand, were married.

Evelyn meanwhile joined Violet at the art school and both soon became successful in the examinations, winning prizes and scholarships for free tuition, but it was their work as book illustrators that brought them the greatest success. Violet at this time entered a competition to design a cover for the new *Studio* magazine and won a prize for her work. She also had a picture included in *A Book of Pictured Carols* which A. J. Gaskin produced with pupils from the Municipal School.

The following year, 1894, Violet and Evelyn, both still under twenty, were invited to help illustrate the fairy story by Blanche Atkinson, *The Real Princess*. Encouraged by this they illustrated their own book of nursery rhymes a year later, which was published by a leading London firm. Evelyn was also delighted when one of her illustrations for

Illustrations by Violet and Evelyn for The House that Jack Built, *the book of nursery rhymes. The sacks in two of the pictures bear the names of Packwood, Lapworth and Bentley Heath, villages near the Holdens.*

AND STRAIGHT IT BEGAN TO PLAY ALONE
BY THE BONNY MILL DAMS O'BINNORIE
O YONDER SITS MY FATHER THE KING
BINNORIE O BINNORIE
AND YONDER SITS MY MOTHER THE QUEEN
BY THE BONNY MILL DAMS OF BINNORIE

This design for stained glass, called "The House that Jack
Built", won Evelyn Holden a prize in 1891 at the Birmingham
Art School's annual exhibition. The design was never
actually made up.

OPPOSITE
Evelyn's illustration for the ballad, "Binnorie, O Binnorie",
chosen for volume 9 of The Yellow Book, which contained
work of students at the Birmingham Art School.
By this time the School had established a reputation
for its book illustrations.

An illustration by Evelyn for The Real Princess *by Blanche Atkinson,
published in 1894. Violet and Evelyn illustrated the book
together. Violet was then twenty-one and Evelyn seventeen.*

This illustration for The House that Jack Built *was
used in a review in* Studio *magazine in 1895. The book
was one of a series for children published by Dent & Co.*

*The Holden annual works picnic c. 1910. Arthur Holden is the bearded man
in the centre front, surrounded by members of his family and firm. Edith
is on his left. All the men are wearing buttonholes,
traditionally picked by the Holden girls from their garden.*

a poem was selected to be published in *The Yellow Book* as
an example of the work of the Birmingham School.

The *Studio* quotes William Morris's remark that "the
only thing that is new strictly speaking [in the Arts and
Crafts Exhibition] is the rise of the Birmingham School of
book decorators". He was impressed with them because
they produced their designs, cut their own blocks and
even printed their own books on occasions, which was
very much in the best tradition of the Arts and Crafts
Movement. So pleased was he with their efforts, that he
lent the school a copy of the *Kelmscott Chaucer*, his own
hand-printed book.

*Amateur dramatics in the garden at Kingswood: Kenneth
Holden (left) fights with Arthur Matthison.
Edith Matthison, Arthur's sister,
also used to participate.*

At Gowan Bank it was always busy. There were often
visitors in the house; any socialist or spiritualist speakers
who came to speak in Birmingham, particularly the visiting Sunday night preacher, were offered the hospitality of
the Holdens' home. Theatrical productions were often put
on in the disused chapel at the side of the garden.

One of those most involved in these dramatic ventures
was Edith's brother Kenneth, who had joined with some
friends to form an amateur dramatic group. Arthur
Matthison, who had joined the firm of Arthur Holden and

*More amateur dramatics: Bernard Holden tends the wounded
Arthur Matthison while Kenneth Holden watches. Productions
were often staged in the garden and Edith Matthison later
became a professional actress.*

Sons and who eventually became joint managing director, was the founder of this group. Edith Wynne Matthison, also a member, went on to become a Shakespearean actress and leading lady to Sir Henry Irving and Beerbohm Tree. Edith Matthison was a close friend of her namesake Edith Holden. They had both been to the Birmingham Art School and had met at various Holden Company events, like the annual works picnic. So the two Matthisons often spent weekends at Gowan Bank enjoying the stimulating literary, socialist or spiritualist discussions, or participating in musical evenings, poetry recitals and theatricals.

CHAPTER

FOUR

WOODSIDE,
DORRIDGE

1897 to 1905

The years at Kingswood had been very enjoyable, with the countryside close at hand for relaxation and the town easily accessible. The house was very large and had been most suitable for entertaining, but as Arthur Holden grew older he felt that somewhere a little smaller was preferable. So in 1897 he took the family to Dorridge, a few miles from Kingswood, to a smaller modern house appropriately called Woodside, at the edge of Dorridge Wood.

The area was still very rural and several miles from Birmingham but with the station at Knowle conveniently near, and it was an area they all knew well from their walks when they lived at Troutbeck and Gowan Bank. Arthur Holden and his wife were both sixty-one at the time of this move. Mrs Holden had been ill for some time and seemed in fact to be getting worse. She spent nearly all her time lying on the chaise-longue in the drawing-room, or when the weather was warm reclining in the garden among her beloved flowers. Her daughter Winnie was a great comfort to her. She had completely taken over the running of the house and the organization of the servants. Winnie was also prepared to sit and read poetry aloud to her mother to help soothe the more painful days or to sit companionably beside her in the garden sketching. On occasions they would discuss poetry or theological issues.

For a long time the Holdens had held weekly seances to which favoured friends and visiting mediums were invited. Mrs Holden was considered to be a particularly good medium herself and appeared to receive messages from various people which she relayed orally or through automatic writing. The daughters participated in various ways. Effie seemed to have more insight into spiritual matters than the other girls and this perhaps gave her inspiration for the poetry which she published after her marriage. Winifred followed her mother in practising automatic writing, while Edith believed in a spirit guide called Hope. Evelyn never really involved herself very much, and said later that it frightened her and that she felt it was best left alone.

*A photograph taken in the late 1890s. In the back row on the left
is Arthur Matthison, third from the left is Kenneth Holden,
then Winifred Holden, a friend of the family, possibly
Mrs Humphreys, and Evelyn Holden; in the front row
third from the left is Arthur Holden with Edith on his
left, and Edith Matthison is on the far right.*

The move to Woodside made no difference to the girls' studies at the art school in Birmingham. After her period in Scotland, Edith returned to work especially on animals, painting them in oils and modelling them. Unable any longer to study Highland cattle at close quarters she turned to dogs and horses, producing various pencil studies of greyhounds and collies, and a modelled design for a frieze with sheep and a dog. She also produced four pictures a year for the exhibitions of the Royal Birmingham Society of Artists. Every year she went to Scotland to stay with Mrs Adam and her son, who had moved from Craigmill to Edinburgh since the death of Denovan Adam Senior, but who still welcomed Edith on her annual visit. She called the six weeks "a holiday" but in reality they were periods of very intensive sketching and painting for her, and provided her with the basis for her exhibition work. In the spring exhibition of 1897 she exhibited *On a Moorland Road, Callander, Perthshire, March Morning: Stirlingshire* and *Perthshire Highlanders* — very typical of her subjects and much influenced by Denovan Adam.

Some of Edith's drawings for Animals Around Us, *a factual book for children on the different sorts of animals.*

Evelyn also began to exhibit at the Royal Birmingham Society of Artists towards the end of the century. Although she had achieved some success as a book illustrator, it was oil paintings of roses and pansies that she produced for exhibition. Oil was not a medium she was happy with and she soon went back to pencil sketches, only occasionally filling them in with watercolours. When she did work in watercolours it was in a much bolder style than Edith, but some of her best work was done in pen and ink.

Violet continued her studies at the art school but did not exhibit her work like her sisters; her speciality was book illustration. The school was making a name for itself in this field under the very able leadership of A. J. Gaskin, and had already published and printed two of its own books of students' work which included some of Violet's work. The *Studio* also mentioned her as one of a rising group of book illustrators at the art school. She continued to win prizes at local and national level for her work and finally in 1904 she joined the teaching staff of the Municipal School of Art, specializing in writing and illumination.

Effie joined her sisters at the Municipal School to further her training in handicrafts, and won a national prize for her "ornament modelled from a cast". But it was particularly in writing poetry that Effie was gaining recognition, although most of her work was printed and circulated privately. She had kept up her correspondence with, but was not yet engaged to, Carl Heath, who by then had qualified as a teacher and was working with a group of other dedicated people in the poorest areas of London, but when his health began to deteriorate he gave this up, and went to Limpsfield in Surrey to teach the children of some friends. The Limpsfield circle was intellectual and artistic, and Effie Holden fitted in easily with them after her marriage to Heath in 1900. She had much to contribute to the group both from her training in handicrafts and her poetry; she often read her work aloud to them.

*A miniature of Emma Wearing, Edith's mother, as a
child of four. She later became a governess,
not marrying until the age of thirty.*

"And Mother takes
the lamp down-
stairs."

Two watercolours by Evelyn intended as book illustrations although they were never published. The style is similar to that of Walter Crane.

Three of Edith's illustrations for Woodland Whisperings, *a collection of poetry for children published in 1911.*

*A watercolour by Edith of a squirrel, taken from a scrapbook
of her work. The date is not known.*

*A watercolour by Winifred Holden taken from a family album.
Unlike her sisters, she never had any art training.*

Earth's increase
foison plenty.
Barns and garners never empty.
Vines with clustering bunches growing.
Plants with goodly burden bowing.
Spring come to you at the farthest.
In the very end of harvest.
Scarcity and want shall shun you:
Honour, riches, marriage blessing.
Long continuance and increasing.
Hourly joys be still upon you...

FEBRUARY
20th
1879.
Aschesté

Another poem composed by Arthur Holden's friend, Aschesté. It is illuminated by Arthur Holden, who has signed it with his monogram.

A watercolour by Evelyn. Her use of colour is bolder than Edith's.

Belbert Cot, Dousland, the Trathen's cottage.
The strange name was made by combining the names of
Bella and Berta Trathen. Edith produced this little watercolour
of the cottage on one of her visits to Dartmoor
and gave it to the Trathen family.

A painting by Edith of Bella.
She made two drawings from
different angles and chose one from
which to do this watercolour.

Picnic at Sheepstor, *a watercolour by Edith of one of the trips she and the Trathen girls had made to this part of Dartmoor in 1907. Edith and Bella are sitting together and Berta is spying over the edge at a neighbour having a picnic below.*

La Proffesseur enragée

A postcard from Edith to Bella, Ernest and Carol which reads, "The angry teacher in search of her lazy pupils." She had started to teach the Trathen children French.

A lively watercolour by Edith,
probably done after her marriage,
taken from a scrapbook of her work.

An undated watercolour by Edith.

A watercolour by Edith from a scrapbook of her work. The date of it is not known, but it is interesting to compare it with the Nature Notes *for July, page 87.*

A watercolour of sheep painted by Edith probably between
1904 and 1910 and given to the Trathens.

A painting by Edith of Jess and her foal, Jan.
Although Edith brought the ponies down to the field behind the
Grange, she painted a moorland background to her picture.

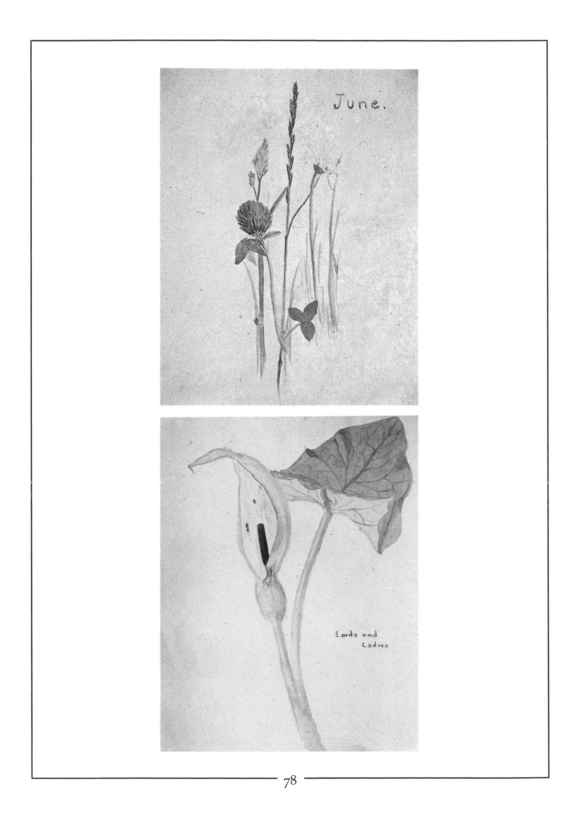

*Some of the work of Doris Hamilton-Smith,
one of Edith's pupils at the Solihull School.
The similarity with Edith's work is apparent:
compare these paintings with Edith's
on pages 64, 76 (shown overleaf)
and 128 of the* Nature Notes.

OVERLEAF
Page 76 of Edith's Nature Notes, *perhaps drawn from the
same specimens as those used by her pupils.*

Orange-tip Butterfly
(Euchloe Cardimines)

Oxe-eye Daisy
(Chrysanthemum leucanthemum)

Purple Clover
(Trifolium pratense)

White or Dutch Clover
(Trifolium répans)

Meadow Fox-Tail Grass
(Alopecurus pratensis)

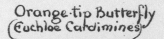

Both Effie and Carl took an active part in all socialist and Fabian debates and became involved in the work of the Humanitarian League. Effie continued all her father's socialist and philanthropic ideas and her commitment to them was even greater than his had been.

Arthur Holden had meanwhile become very involved in the work of the Birmingham Labour Church. Following a similar idea in Manchester, the church had set up an organization called the Cinderella Club, to help the slum children of Birmingham. This club stated that its "work and mission was to bring happiness into the lives of the children of the slums, and to prove that those who are better off than they, both pity and love them". It arranged that the children arrived at half past seven in the evening and were given two buns and two cups of cocoa, followed by games, soup and a fairy tale; at a quarter to nine they would have cocoa and a bun and an apple to take home. From this modest beginning various activities developed as it became increasingly obvious that there was great need among the children of the area.

At Christmas entertainments were staged with magic lantern shows, and various people contributed mince pies, sandwiches and plum puddings for the children's party. Outings were planned for the summer and Arthur Holden had a collecting card whereby members of the family could help by donating money. One of the summer outings at the beginning of the Cinderella Club's history was to the Holdens' garden at Kingswood, but the pattern that developed later was that of taking fifty to sixty children to Sutton Park, north of Birmingham.

One of the organizers wrote: "This may seem a bare programme but one needs to be present to see and feel the happiness it is to the children, their interest in the flowers and plants, to hear their songs and merry shoutings and their cheerings of passing vehicles, cyclists etc., during the ride home."

The Cinderella Club, simply by organizing parties, did not seem to some to be doing enough to alleviate the

*One of the outings to Sutton Park with children from the slums
of Birmingham. Frank Mathews, one of the main organizers,
is third from the left in the back row. The children and
the helpers would travel in furniture vans to this park
north of the town. They arrived about three o'clock and
at half past four cakes and cocoa were served. After
a long ramble and games they would return.*

sufferings of poor children, so its activities were extended
to include "cottage work". As the report for that year
explained, "this cottage work is, we consider, most valu-
able, as the children get an idea of how comfortable a
home can be made with the least amount of expenditure
and they learn in the fortnight naturally more about trees
and flowers and animals than they could in six months in
a Board School."

Arthur Holden was totally convinced of the benefits of
this work and lent his staff cottage for April, May and June

of 1896, which enabled the Cinderella Club to look after a total of thirty-five little invalids at a cottage in the country for a fortnight at a time: "This we have roughly furnished, having installed a caretaker, and are sending batches of four children (boys and girls alternately) for a fortnight's stay, and the good simple food and pure air, works marvels on these poor little mites, who are the most needy little invalids we can find in the slums in Birmingham."

Unfortunately Arthur Holden moved to Woodside the following year and the annual report of the Cinderella Club noted that "through our friend Mr Holden leaving Kingswood early last summer, where he had lent us a cottage free, we had to seek a fresh locality".

One of the important organizers of all this work was Frank Mathews who became a regular visitor at Woodside even though he lived in Lichfield, and had been introduced to the family by Kenneth Holden. They had met on a train journey to Wales and found they had a common philanthropic interest. Knowing that the family would be interested in Frank's work, Kenneth had introduced him at Woodside. The girls were the most interested in his work: they donated money and Evelyn sent a weekly box of flowers from the garden to be distributed among the poor children and sick people.

Frank Mathews before his marriage. He was one of Birmingham's most assiduous workers for the poor and the sick.

Under Frank Mathews's leadership a separate branch of the Cinderella Club was set up which aimed to deal specifically with crippled children in the slums. The Hurst Street Mission, as it was called in 1897 (and the Cripples' Union in 1900), tried to arrange periods of convalescence in the country for crippled children and those recovering from illnesses. The difficulties of finding suitable accommodation were finally overcome in 1900 when the society acquired Chadwick End as a permanent convalescent home for the children.

Chadwick End with a crippled girl sitting in the garden, sketched by Evelyn Holden.

Evelyn's friendship with Frank Mathews developed into love and in October 1902 they became engaged. Evelyn told her mother of this the next morning, but her parents were not as pleased by the match as might be imagined. While admiring Frank's work, they thought so great a commitment could not allow him to give Evelyn the special care they felt she needed.

Evelyn's health had been a constant concern since babyhood, but this was accepted as inevitable in someone so gifted. Arthur Holden believed that people who were artistically sensitive had delicate health; true genius was accompanied by suffering and delicacy came to be almost expected in the members of so talented a family. Edith was perhaps the least concerned by this, commenting in a very matter of fact way: "rode home seven miles in a storm of sleet and snow," along with other accounts of getting soaking wet in her *Nature Notes*. Evelyn was believed to be the most talented of the sisters and so it followed that she would be the most delicate. Ironically she lived longer than any of them, surviving into her nineties.

Mrs Holden wrote to her future son-in-law of her concern: "You know how unusually sensitive she is, how much care she needs in body and spirit." Frank, who regularly saw slum families in appalling conditions, must have found it hard to accept this "artistic preciousness".

Evelyn's parents did come round to accepting the match and Mrs Holden wrote: "You are very similar and you both want to live a simple outward life of help to others and trust in one another, and really you should be very happy." She made a particular plea to Frank not to

OPPOSITE
Chadwick End and some of the convalescent children.
The house was set up in 1900 and run by Frank Mathews and the
Cinderella Club as a place where crippled children or those
recovering from illness could convalesce in the country
away from industrial Birmingham and its slums.

Evelyn Holden in her early twenties.

Evelyn Holden at about the age of forty.

allow Evelyn to become a vegetarian like himself because, she warned, "you will not have her long".

In April 1904 they were married at Newhall Hill Chapel in Birmingham. The ceremony was very simple and quiet because of Mrs Holden's failing health. There was no long white dress for Evelyn, who wore (according to the local newspaper) "a light tweed tailor-made travelling costume". She had her sister Violet as bridesmaid and her brother Bernard as groom.

It was decided to send Rosanna, the old nanny, to live with Evelyn. Although Mrs Holden was by this time obviously dying, it was Winnie and Edith who were nursing her; Rosanna had always given her attention to Evelyn as the youngest child, and it was very fitting that she should go to Bournville a few miles away to live with the newly wedded couple and continue to look after Evelyn.

The last few months of Mrs Holden's life were very sad and difficult for the entire family. Her death from cancer was slow and painful, and she died only a few months after Evelyn's marriage.

Soon after her death, the family believed that Mrs Holden was in touch with them through Winnie. At the end of an essay written for the Central Literary Association's magazine Arthur Holden, using "Senex" as his pseudonym, wrote:

"The following message which was received by 'Senex' from his wife, shortly after her transition, through the automatic writing of one of her daughters, throws an interesting light on the subject we are discussing from the standpoint of the after life.

July 3, 1904

We live in such a little world when we are on earth our sphere of thought is so limited, that when we first come here we are dazzled by the magnitude and extent of everything around us, and it is long before we realize the far reaching effects every thought and act has."

Charles Bernard Holden about 1900. Like Edith, he enjoyed being alone
in the country. At the time of this photograph
he would have been about twenty-five.

Bernard Holden in 1930,
shortly before his death in 1932
at the age of fifty-seven.

The company of Arthur Holden and Sons was going through difficult times. In order for the firm to develop and keep pace with demand, more capital was needed, so it became a limited company with Arthur Holden and his children holding the balance of the shares. At one stage Arthur Holden underwrote a friend's debt and as the friend failed, the money had to be found from the company, so that for six or seven years no dividends were paid. The outside shareholders eventually pressed for a Board of Control to be set up to manage the business in place of the founder who they felt was now too old. The two sons, Kenneth and Bernard, took opposite sides over this issue. Bernard Holden joined forces with Arthur Matthison and Max Sturge, the realistic younger men in the firm, but Kenneth stayed with his father. The Holden girls found themselves in a difficult position being asked to take sides with the two brothers. Edith naturally sided with her father but this brought her into opposition with Evelyn and Violet. The difficulties of the company, besides causing family friction, also caused monetary problems and Arthur Holden began to look around for a smaller house for his family.

Edith found the whole situation very unsettling. Their once very close family seemed to be splitting up, and she began to apply herself with renewed vigour to her painting. She had completed the art courses at the Municipal

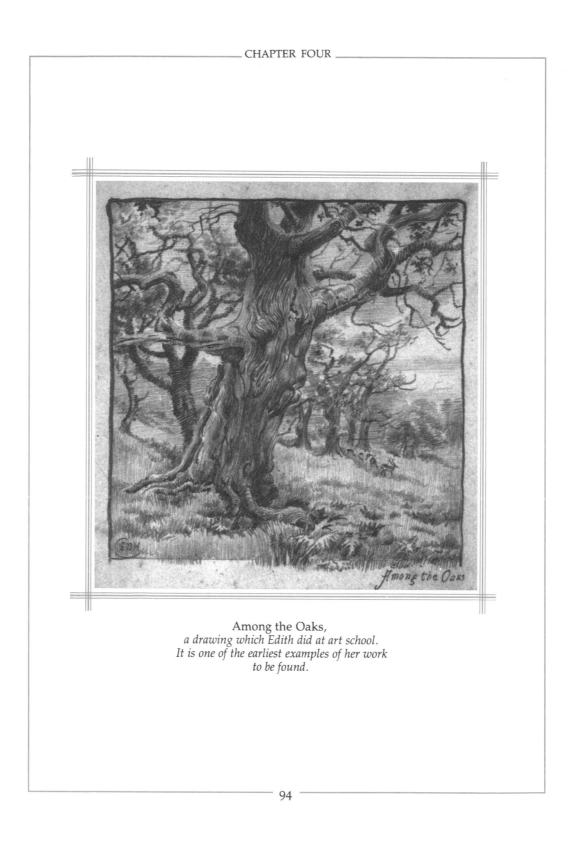

Among the Oaks,
a drawing which Edith did at art school.
It is one of the earliest examples of her work
to be found.

School and now only attended occasionally, concentrating on painting for exhibition.

In 1902 she began to take painting holidays on Dartmoor. This was not an area she knew well since the Holden family usually took their holiday in North Wales.

With its expansive moorland and beautiful valleys, Dartmoor had much in common with her other holiday resorts, and was, as Edith wrote to a friend, "just the kind of country I enjoy myself in".

The journey down, although a long one, was reasonably easy because the Great Western Railway ran direct from Birmingham to Plymouth. Usually the journey was broken with an overnight stay with her aunt Anna, Arthur Holden's sister who had married Charles Townsend and settled in Stoke Bishop near Bristol.

The following day she would continue her journey to Plymouth and from there take the local train which ran through Dousland to Princetown on Dartmoor. It was a beautiful route through the valleys, as Edith wrote in her *Nature Notes*: "Travelled on, to Dousland on Dartmoor. Primroses thick all along the line."

Dousland was a small hamlet that had grown up around the railway station. There were a few cottages and two or three hotels and boarding houses for the growing

*Dousland in the early 1900s, a hamlet on the western edge
of Dartmoor near Tavistock which accommodated the
growing number of summer visitors coming to
Dartmoor by train.*

number of summer visitors. Edith stayed at the Grange, an imposing boarding house that accommodated the "better class of visitor" with its ballroom, tennis courts and croquet lawn.

She stayed in Dousland regularly from 1902 to 1910, usually alone but occasionally accompanied by Winnie. In her *Nature Notes* for 1906 we learn that this was an Easter holiday but she tells us, "I was surprised to find the blue Alkanet already in blossom just where I found it in July last year," and one of the paintings she exhibited in Birmingham was entitled *Wintry Gleam, Dartmoor* which suggests that her visits were not confined to the traditional holiday months.

DOUSLAND GRANGE, YELVERTON.

*The Grange at Dousland on Dartmoor, the boarding house where
Edith stayed. She was usually alone on her
trips to Dartmoor but her sister Winnie sometimes
went with her.*

Quite soon after she started visiting Dousland, Edith
became friendly with the Trathens, a family living near the
Grange, in a cottage called Belbert Cot. This friendship
extended to the whole family and Edith kept up a regular
correspondence with them for many years. The Trathen
children were in their teens when Edith first met them and
found they had a common interest in the countryside and
the wild life of the moorland. The friendship was perhaps
strongest with the two girls, Alberta and Isabella, known
as Berta and Bella, whose names had been combined to
form the name of the cottage, but the three boys, Ernest,
Tom and Carol, also accompanied her on expeditions
across the countryside, and Edith often drew sketches

or wrote comic rhymes to amuse them. Some of the sketches were of members of the family, and these have been treasured by the Trathen family to the present day.

Thomas Trathen the elder was a stone mason who owned a quarry called the South Devon Granite Company. The business varied from carving fonts for local churches to supplying granite for pavements. The Trathens owned several horses which were needed in connection with the business, and one of the sons, Tom, had the daily task of driving out to the quarry with pony and trap to collect the blunted chisels of the previous day, which he took home for sharpening, replacing them with sharp ones. When the pony and trap was not being used at the quarry, Tom drove the visitors at the Grange in a half-governess cart.

A photograph of Bella.

*A drawing by Edith of Bella Trathen, sometimes called Belle,
from which she later did the watercolour. Although Edith
was twenty-nine and Bella only in her teens when
they first met, they became good friends and
corresponded for many years.*

A drawing by Edith, thought to be of Alberta Trathen.
Like Edith, the two Trathen girls were interested in the wildlife
and countryside of Dartmoor where they lived and it was
this common interest which prompted Edith's friendship
with them and then with the whole family.

Thomas Trathen the elder with one of the fonts produced by his company from local stone. He was a stone mason and owned a granite quarry. His eldest son, Thomas, also worked for the company.

*A drawing by Edith of Mrs Anne Trathen. Mrs Trathen ran
Dousland Post Office from the family's cottage with the
help of her two daughters.*

OPPOSITE
Carol Trathen as a boy, drawn by Edith.
The family consisted of three boys and two girls
and Carol was the youngest.

Edith loved the animals owned by the Trathens and quite soon knew their names. In her letters she always remembered them. Her painting of Rob Roy, the Great Dane, is still in the family's possession.

Mrs Trathen and her two daughters ran the Dousland Post Office at Belbert Cot. The visitors to the Grange had previously to go a few miles down the road to Yelverton to buy a stamp and to avoid this inconvenience Mrs Trathen agreed to open the local Post Office. Berta, Bella and their mother had to go to Yelverton to be sworn in by the Post Office and the two girls admitted afterwards that they found it very hard to stop giggling throughout the pompous ceremony.

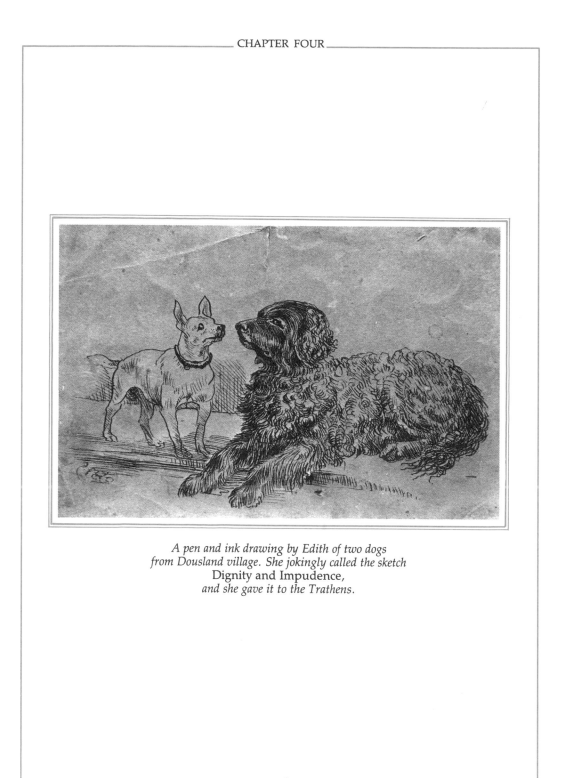

*A pen and ink drawing by Edith of two dogs
from Dousland village. She jokingly called the sketch*
Dignity and Impudence,
and she gave it to the Trathens.

When the girls were not working they often went walking with Edith on Yennadon Down behind Dousland. She described it: "Up on the moor the world seemed to be made up of sky and gorse — such acres of fragrant golden blossom under a sky of cloudless blue." The two girls showed Edith other favourite walks and one of their trips to Sheepstor was delightfully recorded on a postcard which she sketched and sent to them later in the year. She also drew sketches of the birds they saw and gave them to the girls, and on another occasion she drew two local dogs which she called *Dignity and Impudence*. Much of her correspondence to the family was written on the back of sketches the size of postcards.

During her visits to the Grange Edith began to teach French to some of the Trathen children and when she returned home she sent them exercises by post. One of her letters to Carol, written in French, reads: "Do you think that your teacher had forgotten you altogether? I have been very busy, but now that the winter has come, I hope that you will have a bit more time to study French. I will do my best to help you ... Goodbye, be a good boy and do the little exercise that I am sending you."

As the Trathen family got to know Edith better so her correspondence included more personal details like reports of the annual works picnic, or anecdotes of her family. They in return wrote telling her of their various exploits, which we can only guess at from her replies: "What an exciting time you must have had with that hare! — Great fun for you but how about the hare!"

To Belle

There was a young lady called Belle
Who looked so uncommonly well
All the maidens in vain
Tried to dress just the same
But they never could rival fair Belle.

Wishing you
a happy Christmas
from Edith Holder.

*Part of a Christmas card from Edith to Bella Trathen.
The comic verse is written by Edith but she did not
include one of her own paintings here.*

To Berta

There was a young maiden called Berta
The sun and the rain could not hurt her.
They kissed her soft hair,
and her forehead so fair
And they brightened the eyes of sweet Berta

With best wishes
from Edith Holden

A card to Berta painted by Edith,
with a comic verse composed by her,
probably for Berta's birthday.

The friendship was much cherished on both sides, and birthdays and Christmas were always remembered. Edith drew and painted a card for each of the children at Christmas and when she sent a photograph she was careful to include one each.

When she returned from Dartmoor after her holiday in 1905 it was to prepare for yet another move, this time to a house in Olton.

CHAPTER
FIVE

GOWAN BANK, OLTON

OLTON

1906

The Year of Nature Notes

*Gowan Bank, Olton, from the front, in 1920. The family lived
here from 1905 until Arthur Holden moved to Letchworth in 1911.
It was here, in 1906, that Edith wrote the* Nature Notes.

*Gowan Bank, Olton, from the garden at the back c.1920. Edith says
in the* Nature Notes *for March, "Tonight a Toad was
discovered jumping about in the hall; it must have
come in through the garden door which has been
standing open all day."*

Arthur Holden was sixty-nine when the family moved to
Olton in the summer of 1905 where he rented one of four
houses which had recently been built in Kineton Green
Road and which they called Gowan Bank. This house was
smaller than any of their previous ones, but it was ideal for
the diminishing family and less affluent times.

Edith and her father were joined by Winifred and
Violet, but Bernard, the younger son, who had lived with
them at Dorridge, by this time had left for some lodgings of
his own in the country. Business relations with his father

and his brother Kenneth had become strained, and Bernard, who was a quiet man, much preferred the peace of the country and playing his violin to the pressures of industry. He was well liked and respected by people like Arthur Matthison and Edith Wynne Matthison, who admired his extensive knowledge and gentlemanly manner.

The living space in the house was considerably reduced, with three bedrooms on the first floor, and rooms for the servants on the top floor. The staff had decreased over the year, so that at Olton they only had their maid Florence living in and relied more on daily help. Florence had been with them for quite a few years by that stage and it seemed natural to retain her to cook and keep house for them. The rest of the staff consisted of a Mrs Jones who came in to do the laundry once a week, another woman who came daily for the cleaning and a man a couple of days a week to work in the garden.

Like the house, the garden was smaller than previous ones but nevertheless the girls took great interest and care in planning it, with gooseberry bushes, sunflowers and as Edith tells us in her *Nature Notes*, "Primroses, Polyanthus, Winter Aconite, Mazereon and Snowdrops". A walnut tree was also planted which gradually grew to shade some of the lawn in summer.

Olton was closer to Birmingham than the previous Holden residences but retained much of its rural character even though it was growing as a commuter village. As she records in her *Nature Notes*, Edith was able to walk down many lanes and across many fields. We know a good deal about Edith's activities in 1906 because we are fortunate in having her own diary. It is specifically concerned with nature, but occasionally there are little pieces of other information contained within it. For instance, we learn from it that Edith had a very good friend in Knowle (Knowle and Dorridge were used as interchangeable names by Edith; she gave her address sometimes as one, sometimes the other during her time at Woodside), whom she cycled to see every Saturday but tantalizingly she never reveals the person's name.

Although they moved in the late summer of 1905, Edith did not start her *Nature Notes* until the beginning of the next year. She was at pains to list all the varieties of birds and flowers found in this new area. For some of her information she had to rely on neighbours as she was newly arrived, and when commenting on a strangely coloured robin she says, "I hear that it was seen about here last summer."

At the very beginning of the year in her *Nature Notes*, Edith concentrated on walking around the local countryside and discovering many of its charms. She found the violet wood and the daffodil field, and her accounts have all the freshness and excitement of a new discovery.

At other times Edith cycled back to the district she had recently come from and revisited her favourite haunts. In July she went to a place called Balsall Temple, which she must have visited frequently in her days at Kingswood. She comments: "I knew the Wild Canterbury Bell (Creeping Campanula) used to grow by the stream there, years ago and I was anxious to find it again, nor was I disappointed." However she went "to search for the Spreading Campanula, where it used to grow years ago, but all trace of it had disappeared".

Soon after she moved to Olton, Edith became friendly with the sister of the vicar of Shirley, the Rev E. Burd.

*The Solihull School for Girls, near Olton, where Edith taught
art on Friday afternoons from 1906 to 1909. It was a
private school for about forty pupils run by a
friend of Edith's, Miss Burd.*

Miss Burd ran a private school for about forty girls in
Solihull and early in 1906 Edith agreed to go and teach art
there on Friday afternoons.

Although it was a girls' school there were a few boys,
brothers of the older girls, in the nursery. Most of the
pupils came in daily from the surrounding areas, although
there were a few weekly boarders. About five girls lived in
right at the top of the school house with the science and
literature mistresses. Miss Burd was a strict headmistress
and most of the girls were frightened of her. As a special
treat she sometimes took one or two of the older girls to
tea with her brother at the vicarage, which was always a
very formal affair. She was very keen on games and the
girls even had their own cricket team and played away

The ford near Bushwood; Edith says in the Nature *Notes for March: "Cycled to the withy-beds within half a mile of Bushwood . . . I had to carry my cycle nearly a quarter of a mile down a steep, muddy ford . . ."*

against schools in Warwick as well as in other parts of Birmingham.

It was arranged that Edith should come and teach the older girls, who ranged from fourteen to seventeen years old. Miss Burd had encouraged the girls to keep diaries recording the changing seasons and to link their work with suitable passages from literature, and Edith felt that she could fit her Friday afternoon lesson in to this scheme by bringing appropriate specimens of flowers, twigs or berries for the girls to draw. With pressed exhibits and photographs, the nature diaries would record the observations of each girl throughout the year.

Miss Burd gave out note-books to the girls and appropriate verses to start them off, but she informed them that in the future they must select their own material. She also added that when Miss Holden came they would do suitable drawings.

The girls found Edith reserved and reticent about herself. She had fairish hair drawn back and usually wore a high-necked blouse and long skirt. She had a very quiet personality and never belittled anyone's efforts, but she demanded high standards from her pupils.

Each week Edith collected specimens of the chosen plant and brought them in for her pupils. She gave one to each to draw, and would then wander round from girl to girl advising and correcting while they worked. When a

A photograph of Mr and Mrs Trathen and Carol in a trap pulled by Jess,
one of the family's Dartmoor ponies. They had three ponies
which were used by the family at home and at the quarry and also
for driving the guests at the Grange.

sketch was approved the young artist could go on to paint
it. If there wasn't enough time to complete the painting in
the lesson, Edith brought some more examples of the
specimen the following week. Everything had to be
finished off properly and labelled before it was acceptable,
and although this was tiresome, the girls respected her for
her teaching methods and grew to like her quiet manner.

It is known that Edith herself painted in her *Nature
Notes* specimens which were given to her pupils in class.
In her entry for Wednesday 16th May Edith noted, ''This
afternoon I went to gather Cuckoo-pints for my drawing
class.'' These she wrapped carefully in paper and laid in
her basket, then brought them to school on her bicycle.

Kineton Road
Olton
Nr Birmingham
Nov. 20th

Dear Bella

How do you like the Birming-
-ham coat of arms? I am
afraid the Birmingham motto
has been 'Backward' lately
not 'Forward' in politics at
any rate. I hope you are
keeping better, I suppose
it is very quiet at Dous-
-land now, all the visitors
will be leaving; that is the
just the time I should like
to be there. Many thanks for
your letter and love to you and
all; from yours affecty
E.B.H.

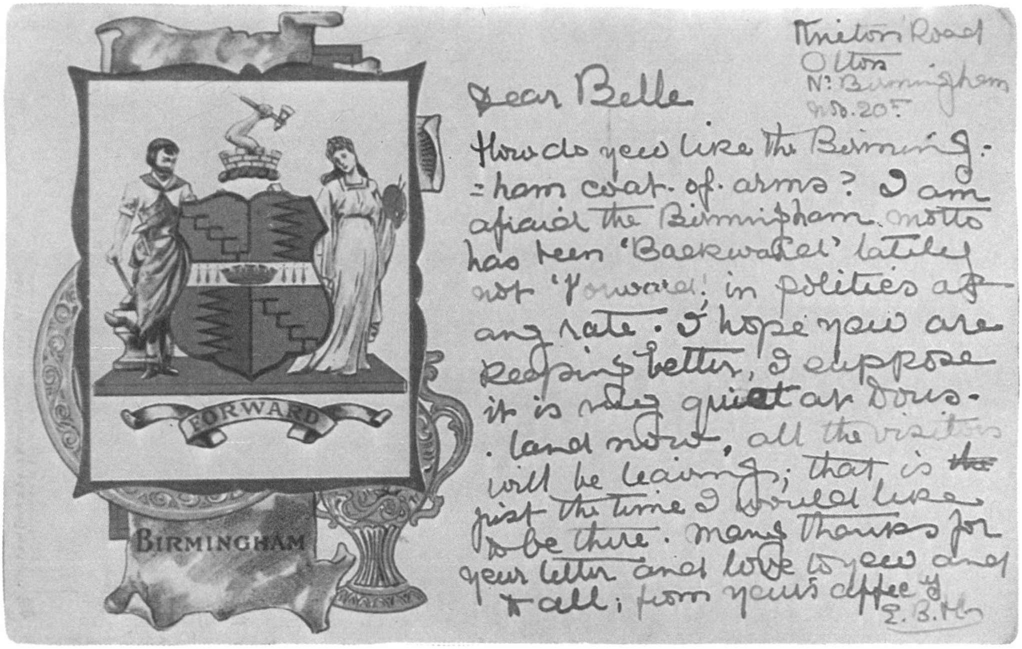

A postcard with the Birmingham coat of arms from Edith to Bella in November 1906. Edith bewails the fact that she is in Birmingham and not in Dousland, particularly at the time of year when all the summer visitors will have gone.

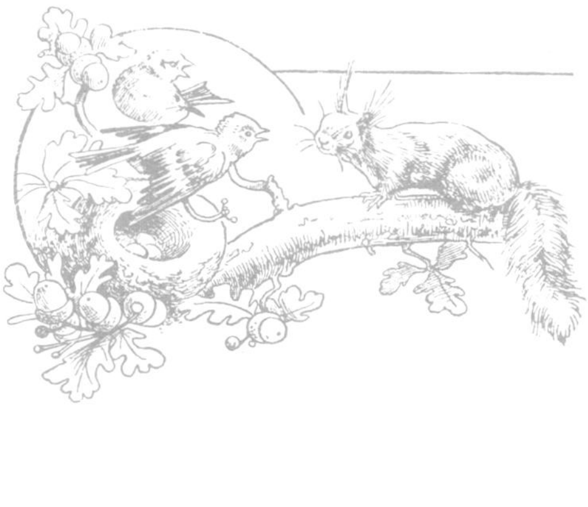

At the end of the lessons, homework was set. Sometimes Miss Holden specified that it should be a figure-drawing or a still life, but more usually she allowed them to draw what they liked and the girls often resorted to copying pictures from books.

As time passed, the girls progressed from drawing plants in the classroom to going out into the very extensive school grounds to sketch the schoolhouse or views of Solihull Church.

Edith also participated in other school activities, such as helping the girls to prepare for the annual garden party in July to which parents and friends of the school were invited. Invitations had to be designed and executed by the girls and souvenirs made for presentation to each parent after the event. Edith chose Doris Hamilton-Smith, one of her more able pupils, to paint a design on to material for one of these souvenirs.

Edith taught at the Solihull School for Girls for about four years, and by the time she left she had become a personal friend of Miss Burd, who was encouraged by her commitment to the school and her interest in her pupils' work. It was a rewarding and productive period of her life.

Edith spent Easter of 1906 on Dartmoor and continued her close friendship with the Trathens. The day after her arrival at the Grange she writes: "In the afternoon I went up on to the moor to bring home a pony and foal. Both are delightfully picturesque in their shaggy winter coats and I hope to begin their portraits tomorrow morning." The pony was her old friend Jess who, harnessed to a trap, had taken Edith out on previous visits. She was delighted to see the new foal Jan who had been born since her last visit and to hear news of little Jan's training the following year in a letter from Berta. In reply she commented: "Fancy little Jan running in the cart."

Another painting which Edith exhibited also had its origin in this Dartmoor holiday: *Study of Chaffinch's Nest and Hawthorns.* The exhibition work was in oils, but Edith produced a study for it which she uses as her title page for May in her *Nature Notes.* The original nest seems to have been discovered that Easter Sunday on Dartmoor, as she recorded: "found a Chaffinch's nest nearly finished in a young Hawthorn."

She exhibited the *Study of a Hedge-Sparrow's Nest* at the same time as her *Study of a Chaffinch's Nest and Hawthorns.*

She left Dartmoor at the beginning of May and travelled back to Olton by the Great Western Railway, again staying overnight with the Townsends. During her time in Dousland she became friendly with other members of the community who knew of her interest in nature. In her *Nature Notes* Edith records something which Miss Burnett, a local resident, showed her: "Miss B. had some lovely Pasque Flowers sent her from Oxfordshire this morning." Someone knowing her interest in birds helped her: "A native of Dousland showed me a bank covered with gorse and briars, where he said he was sure a Bramble Finch was building, I only know this bird by reputation, so mean to go again and watch for it."

Her remarks to Bella in November of 1906 give us an idea of this quiet person who was happy to cycle for miles alone, when she said: "I suppose it is very quiet at Dousland now, all the visitors will be leaving, that is just the time I would like to be there."

The Solihull School for Girls in 1908. On the far left in the back row is Miss Burd, the headmistress. Doris Hamilton-Smith, one of Edith's most promising pupils is fourth right in the row second from the front.

After her return from Dartmoor life carried on much as normal for Edith, with regular Saturday morning visits to Knowle and art classes on Friday afternoons. In June she went on an outing "with a large party" and listed the places they drove through which had a special interest because they were in an area she knew well from her former days at Kingswood. The group she was with contained others who were interested in nature and together they observed several butterflies and birds' nests.

Edith evidently enjoyed the warm days of early summer, commenting on several occasions: "Glorious day with cloudless sky and bright sunshine all day long." Her entries for June and July are full of such vivid accounts of the flowers and butterflies that anyone reading them cannot help but feel they are there with her when she writes of "tall purple foxgloves and nodding heads of grasses heavy with pollen".

The school in Solihull finished for the summer holidays at the end of July and Edith went by herself to Scotland.

The West Highland Railway: Callander Station about 1900.
The line ran through superb and unspoilt countryside, and
Edith was able to travel from Callander to the coast.

Earlier that year Mrs Adam had taken over the running of
a small boarding house called Inverteith, on the edge of
Callander close to the foothills of the Trossachs with
breath-taking views on clear mornings.

Edith loved the area perhaps even better than that
around Craigmill, because from Callander she could explore the countryside around the lochs or high on the
hills. Always it was quiet and beautiful. It was also an area
very closely linked with literature and steeped in history.
Edith investigated with great interest the local traditions
about Rob Roy, walking out to see the legendary tomb and
reading the heroic tale, but it was Sir Walter Scott's
connection with the area which really fired her imagina-
tion. She knew *The Lady of the Lake* well and the Waverley
novels, and on her earlier visits to Callander she had spent
many days travelling to the places she knew from her
reading.

*The High Street, Callander, in the early 1900s. After the death
of Denovan Adam his wife had taken over a small boarding
house in the town and Edith used to go to stay there.
She loved the area and spent her time exploring the hills
and lakes by foot, bicycle and boat.*

Some of the lines she quoted from *The Lady of the Lake*
turned out to be more apt than she might have hoped.

So darkly looms yon thunder-cloud
That swathes as with a purple shroud
Ben-ledi's distant hill.

The weather was miserable, the distant peak of Ben-ledi
seemed permanently hidden by rain-clouds. In a card to
Bella Trathen soon after her arrival Edith wrote: "Had lots
of rain and haven't done any painting yet." Unfortunately
the weather did not change and at the end of the month
she commented in *Nature Notes:* "There has been almost
continuous rain in Scotland this month, although in
England it has been one of the sunniest months on
record."

Nevertheless she disregarded the weather as much as
possible and began sketching as well as just visiting places

for pleasure. In previous years she had visited the well-known tourist sights and on this occasion had promised herself a visit to Oban, which was very easy to accomplish because the West Highland Railway ran from Callander to Oban through the most beautiful scenery, and she noted "quantities of wild flowers all along the route".

After a few days she settled down to sketching in earnest. She always worked well in Scotland. Perhaps it was because her most intensive art training had been in this setting that she felt so at home with it. Edith went out on several days to sketch and paint some Highland cattle, those great favourites of Denovan Adam. Her description in *Nature Notes* could easily have fitted a day at Craigmill:

> As I was walking across the fields to the
> cattle today, a Snipe flew up from the
> grass at my feet, soon after I saw a curlew
> alight in the field. There were numbers
> of Starlings running round the cattle as
> they were feeding, following the animals
> all round the field, they seemed to be
> picking up the insects, disturbed by the
> animals in browsing.

On days when she had a rest from sketching, she enjoyed herself taking picnics and walking or rowing round the lochs. With a friend she borrowed a bicycle and they were able to explore quite a long way from Callander. This must have been very strenuous, because Edith cycled as many as forty miles on occasions up steep hills through the Trossachs.

On this occasion she revisited the Lake of Menteith with its little islands and historic connections. She walked to Menteith with a companion, the round trip being about twelve miles, and they had lunch at the Lake Hotel. Edith was intrigued by the large pike for which the lake was famous: "the walls of the little inn-parlour on the edge of the lake are hung round with fine stuffed specimens in cases." The hotel hired out rowing boats, and they took one for a trip over to one of the islands.

There are two islands in the Lake of Menteith, the smaller one with a ruined castle and the larger, which they chose to visit, with the ruins of Inchmahome Priory, where the five-year-old Mary Queen of Scots had once taken refuge. Edith described the island in her *Nature Notes*:

> Here were huge old Spanish Chesnut [sic]
> Trees supposed to have been planted by
> the monks, and the largest Nut trees I
> have ever seen; also the Box tree, said
> to have been planted by Queen Mary. Most
> of the Chesnut were green and vigorous,
> with wonderful, twisted trunks and
> covered with fruit, as were the Nut trees.
> The ruined walls of the Priory were green
> with the tiny Wall Spleenwort, and
> Harebells were waving their purple bells
> aloft from many of the top most crevices.

After an interesting walk around the island, they rowed back to the inn, and returned to Callander over the hills. Edith observed "the colours of some of the mosses and bog plants were very vivid, the orange seed-vessels of the Asphodel, and deep crimson, and palest of pale green, mosses being particularly striking. The heather is all turning brown now, — only a bit pink here and there."

When they returned from a day by Loch Vennachar they "witnessed a wonderful sunset across the water. The reflected light on the Eastern hilltops was gorgeous — all shades of gold and red and brown, deepening into purple and grey shadows at the base of the mountains."

The holiday soon passed. Denovan Adam the younger was now a young man painting and exhibiting in his own right. He remembered Edith with affection from the days when he had been ill and she had spent much of her spare time trying to amuse him. She returned to Craigmill, now inhabited by another artist, and to Cambuskenneth, meeting again some of the artists she had known from her student days.

She arrived home in time to celebrate her thirty-fifth birthday in Olton, and to begin the autumn term at Solihull School.

The holiday in Scotland had been a pleasant break. After her return, Edith worked on the painting of Highland cattle which she planned to exhibit the following spring under the title of *Moorland Pasture*. For the autumn exhibition in Birmingham, Edith had already completed *Dartmoor Ponies*. Her previous year's entry, *The Rowan Tree*, had been very well received, and like many of her other paintings, this one had been inspired by her visits to Scotland.

Various people brought objects for Edith to sketch. Effie "sent me some lovely crimson toad stools with white spots, this morning, from Keston Common. Though a good deal damaged by the journey, all the heads of the toad stools being severed from their stems, I managed to make a sketch of one or two."

The weather became very snowy at the end of the year so Edith stayed at home watching the birds which came to feed in the garden, and waiting for the thaw after the hardest winter of the new century.

CHAPTER

SIX

OLTON AND
LONDON

1907 to 1920

After 1906 we do not have the advantage of Edith's *Nature Notes*, which provide such an insight into her life. The notes were never repeated but they remained a very useful portfolio of her work. In the following years Edith often returned to her diary to borrow material or adapt an idea to suit a new purpose.

She prepared a calendar right at the beginning of 1907 based very much on her *Nature Notes*. Many of the illustrations are readily recognizable, and the use of mottoes and quotations can clearly be seen to have come from it, but a careful study shows that they are all directed towards care for animals. Edith's interest in animals led her to belong to the National Council for Animals' Welfare and she designed this calendar for their magazine *The Animals' Friend*. From April 1907 through to March 1908 a page of her calendar appeared monthly. The calendar was also produced commercially and sold in aid of the charity at the end of 1907 ready for the new year. Edith decided to send it to her friends in Dousland, with her usual hand-drawn Christmas card. Although it was produced in sepia, and not in the vivid colours of the *Nature Notes*, it is nevertheless a charming piece of work. It began an association between Edith and *The Animals' Friend* which lasted for five years. During this time she contributed some forty illustrations to the magazine.

For Edith 1907 was a busier year than the previous one, both in terms of travelling and of painting. Early in the year she stayed with friends in Castle Bromwich, near Birmingham, and then later in the spring she went to Norfolk with her father, two sisters and brother Kenneth. He had been ill for some time and it was felt that the change would do him good. Edith wrote with great excitement to her friends about her journey through the King's park and her view of Sandringham.

In between these visits she managed to exhibit a painting at the Royal Birmingham Society of Artists' spring exhibition. *A Moorland Pasture* was the last painting she ever exhibited in Birmingham, and she had already decided to offer her painting, *The Rowan Tree*, for the Royal Academy summer exhibition.

The frequent visits to London to stay with her sister Effie had widened Edith's horizons both socially and artistically. Effie and Carl were active members of various humane movements like the Christian Socialist Society, the Fellowship of New Life (which developed into the Fabian Society), the Humanitarian League and the Society for the Abolition of Capital Punishment. Carl was a teacher at this time, but he and Effie felt strongly that he should be doing some full-time humanitarian work. So in 1909 he successfully applied for the post of Secretary to the National Peace Council. Edith found herself very much in sympathy with the aims of Carl and Effie. Effie also continued to write and publish volumes of poetry, which led her to correspond with and meet some of the leading literary figures of the day.

Edith found their life fascinating. So much seemed to be happening in London compared with her quiet existence in the country. Of her four sisters, Edith had been closest to Effie. They were near in age and shared common interests, and although Effie had moved away quite early on, Edith had kept in regular correspondence. Effie usually returned to the family for Christmas and annual holidays in Wales.

FOLLOWING PAGES
Pages from the calendar produced by Edith in 1907,
originally for The Animals' Friend. *The calendar was in sepia*
and not colour, but many of the illustrations are similar to those
in the Nature Notes. *She sent a copy of it to the Trathens.*

MARCH

If children at school can be made to understand

how it is just and noble to be humane, even to what we term inferior animals, it will do much to give them a higher tone and character through life. John Bright

Primrose

Lesser Celandine

Sweet Violet

Song Thrush

Oh, leave them in the wilderness,
Or in the bush, or in the brake;
Let them in liberty possess
The haunts God fashioned
For their ———— sake!

And all the glories of their throats
Shall sound more glorious
When they rise
In flights and waves of noble notes
To stir your hearts
And dim your eyes.

Norman Gale

Daffodils

Blackbird and nest

JULY

Tufted Vetch

And Nature, the old nurse, took
The child upon her knee,
Saying: "Here is a story-book
Thy Father hath written for thee.
Longfellow
Sweet mercy is nobility's true badge.
Shakespeare

Red Admiral
Butterfly

Blackberry
blossom

Yellow
Vetchling

Kingfisher

Scarlet
Poppy

Great Dragonfly

If to do good is to generate
welfare, then to cause welfare to
a horse, a bird, a butterfly, or a
fish, is to do good just as truly as
to cause welfare to men. Howard Moore.

Frog

White and Yellow
Water Lillies

SEPTEMBER

Rowan or Mountain Ash Berries

I doubtna, whiles, but thou may thieve:
What then? poor beastie, thou maun live!
A daimen icker in a thrave
    'S a sma' request:
I'll get a blessing wi' the lave,
    And never miss't.
                    Robert Burns

Greenfinch feeding on Elderberries

Harvest Mice and Nest

Who taught the natives of the field and flood
To shun their poison and to choose their food?
                    Pope

"Man has nothing that the beasts have not at least a vestige of; the animals have nothing that man does not in some degree share.
                    Seton Thompson

Blackberries

Fruit of Horse Chesnut

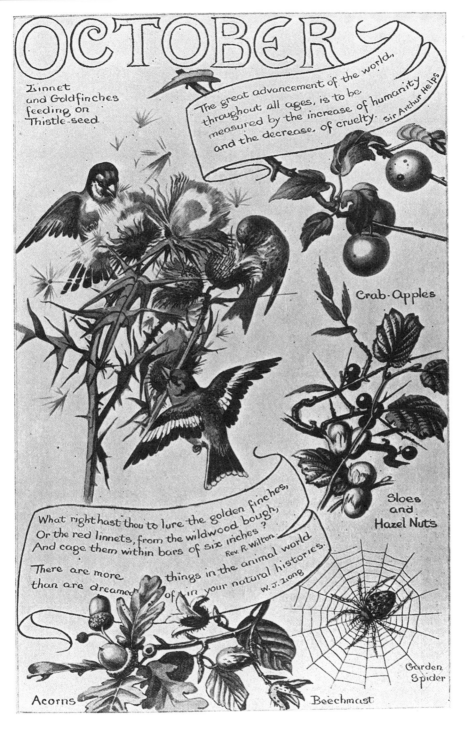

OCTOBER

Linnet and Goldfinches feeding on Thistle-seed.

The great advancement of the world, throughout all ages, is to be measured by the increase of humanity and the decrease of cruelty. Sir Arthur Helps

Crab-Apples

Sloes and Hazel Nuts

What right hast thou to lure the golden finches,
Or the red linnets, from the wildwood bough,
And cage them within bars of six inches?
Rev. R. Wilton.

There are more things in the animal world than are dreamed of in your natural histories.
W. J. Long

Acorns

Beechmast

Garden Spider

Feb. 6th 1907

Under the snow, Love,
Under the snow,
Lieth a flower, Love.,
Sleeping below.
So, in the heart, Love,
Silent today,
Lieth a song, Love,
Hidden away.

And as the wind, Love,
Wooing the lea,
Bidding the flower, Love,
Burgeon and be.
So to the heart, Love,
Cometh a voice
Bidding the song, Love,
Live and rejoice.

Till on a day, Love,
Lo, as you pass,
Gallant and gay, Love,
Down in the grass.
Look at the star, Love,
Silver and gold
Red at the rim, Love,
Blushing and bold.

And in the heart, Love,
All on a day,
Carols a bird, Love,
Hidden away,
Carolling joy, Love,
Carolling sweet;
Carolling close, Love,
Close to your feet. e.m.c.

ABOVE AND OPPOSITE
A postcard from Edith to Bella on her birthday in February
1907. The poem is illuminated by Edith and the border of
flowers is an idea she had used the year before to decorate
poetry in the Nature Notes.

When Edith stayed in London, the two sisters visited exhibitions, galleries, attended meetings together, or walked in the parks. Edith made many new friends, and one of these was a sculptor, Ernest Smith, who was studying at the Royal College of Art. He was a bearded young man with chestnut hair and a friendly nature and their friendship developed gradually as Edith spent more time in London.

Edith continued teaching at Solihull School and in addition to the Friday afternoon lessons she also taught one of the most talented pupils, Doris Hamilton-Smith, privately for one morning a week. While the other Holden daughters subscribed to the Cripples' Union, the Church Building Fund and other such causes, Edith regularly sent money to the Royal Society for the Prevention of Cruelty to Animals. She began to do artwork for them, producing several pen and ink sketches of animals which were made into postcards to be sold for the charity.

*One of Edith's postcards produced about 1907 for the
Royal Society for the Prevention of Cruelty to Animals.
She regularly sent the Society donations and designed
several of their postcards.*

At the end of the summer term in 1907, Edith wrote to Bella Trathen, "It really seems as if I were coming to Dousland this Summer," and by the beginning of August she had arrived there. She stayed this year as a most welcome guest of the Trathen family at Belbert Cot.

After her return she worked on a book in collaboration with Effie. They wanted to produce a book together, with Effie's poetry and Edith's illustrations, remembering perhaps the way Evelyn and Violet had worked together earlier. But Effie's poetry was not easily combined with Edith's drawings of animals. For this enterprise they produced a very small book of animal poems designed for children called *Birds, Beasts and Fishes*, with poems by two other contributors, Ann and Jane Taylor.

The title page of
Birds Beasts and Fishes.

Edith at about the time of her marriage,
one of the few portraits in existence.

*A photograph of Carol Trathen in his World War I uniform.
He died not long afterwards. When Edith first knew him he
was only a young boy.*

At Christmas Edith, in a birthday letter to her young
friend Carol Trathen, told him of her activities:

Gowan Bank
Kineton Road
Olton

21st December 1907

My dear Carol

I must not forget your birthday in the midst of all the
correspondence that Christmas brings with it. I can't quite
remember just how many years old you are — is it fourteen
or fifteen? but however many years it may be, I hope you
will have a very happy birthday and very many happy
returns of the day and lots of good health and good spirits
in the new year you are just beginning.

I hope you will all have a very merry Christmas all
together; I shall think of you all and just wish I could pop
in and see you for dinner-time on Christmas day. I should
like to see you all dressed up in the paper caps etc. I was at
a supper-party the other night; and we had crackers and

every guest had a lovely bunch of violets placed by her
seat. All the ladies put on their crowns and dunce's caps
and mob-caps; one lady looked especially comic in a
fire-man's helmet.

Please thank Belle for her pretty card; you seem to have
been having very much the same kind of weather that we
have been favoured with; — gales of wind and rain that
nearly washed us away. I can imagine the mud that lies
between your house and the front gate!

We are all jogging along much as usual; *next* week we
shall be busy; Mr and Mrs Heath are coming from London
for a week; and very likely my friend Mr Smith will be
spending Christmas with us. Tell your Mother I am
wearing the lovely present she sent me — and they are so
warm and comfortable. She will be interested to hear that
my eldest brother — the one who has been ill for so long, is
much better now, and he is going abroad after Christmas
with another gentleman. They are going to Algiers and will
probably be away till March. So I hope that will complete
the cure. How is dear old Rob? and how is Jess, and Mollie
and Joey? Please give my love to them all: I hope you will
all like the pictures of a certain person that I am sending
you. I feel I ought to apologise for sending so many to one
household; and I hope you will put some of them away out
of sight. I know you all like to have your own of
everything: and you have all given me so many photos; I
felt glad to be able to make some return. You see I
promised somebody to get my photograph taken before
Christmas; and so all my friends are getting the benefit of
them now. My dear little boy, I must say goodbye, with
the best of good wishes and much love to you all.

Ever yours affectionately,
Edith Holden.

Soon after Christmas, Edith was in bed with influenza and
all her correspondence ceased. She had no paintings to
exhibit in the 1908 spring exhibition at Birmingham,
although she had successfully exhibited at the Royal
Academy. She also had two paintings accepted by the

A postcard from Edith to Bella in February 1908, sent from Olton.
Edith was living at home although she was by this
time thirty-seven. She was still writing to the Trathens
eight years after they had first met.

Walker Gallery in Liverpool and later one by the Society of Women Artists.

She went again to London in the summer of 1908 but as Carl and Effie were in France, Edith stayed with Miss Spence-Bate, a friend in Kensington. To Bella she wrote, "I have left Olton for a week or two and am enjoying myself I can tell you. The parks here are beautiful, I never saw such flowers. I am going to the White City on Monday. We are having lovely weather. Only one wet day since I came. Mr and Mrs Heath have been in France — came back to London yesterday I think. So I hope to see them. Much love to you all. Wish I was coming on to Dartmoor when I leave here."

THE FORD, OLTON.

A card Edith sent to Bella in May 1908,
with a view of the ford at Olton, near Gowan Bank.
On it she says the ford is about ten minutes'
walk from their house.

An oil painting by Edith of the Trathens' Great Dane, Rob Roy, which she gave to them.

*A Christmas card painted in watercolour by Edith, sent
from Olton to the Trathens. It shows a Scottish scene.*

RIGHT
Page 108 from the Nature Notes, *painted by Edith
in Scotland near Callander.*

OVERLEAF
Pages 79 and 80 from Edith's Nature Notes, *for June.
She says on the 16th, "The Roses and Honeysuckle are
full of bud, but they are late in bloom this year . . . "*

AUGUST

79.

'The pleachèd bower'
Where honeysuckles, ripened by the sun,
Forbid the sun to enter. '
                    'Much Ado' Shakespeare.

'All twinkling with t
The briar-rose fa

'For the Rose, ho, the Rose! is the eye of the flowers,
    Is the blush of the meadows that feel themselves fair,
    Is the lightning of beauty that strikes thro' the bowers,
On pale lovers who sit in the glow unaware.
Ho, the Rose breathes of love! ho, the Rose lifts the cup
    To the red lips of Cypris invoked for a guest!
Ho! the Rose, having curled it's sweet leaves for the world,
    Takes delight in the motion it's petals keep up
        As they laugh to the wind, as it laughs
        from the west ! '
                        E.B.B. Trans. from Sappho

Dog Roses (Rosa canina)
Honey suckle (Lonicera caprifolium)

ewdrop's sheen
streamers green?
Scott

*A watercolour of swallows taken from a scrapbook
of Edith's work.*

A Christmas card to the Trathens from Edith.
The painting shows two field mice with a poppy,
harebells and ox-eye daisies.

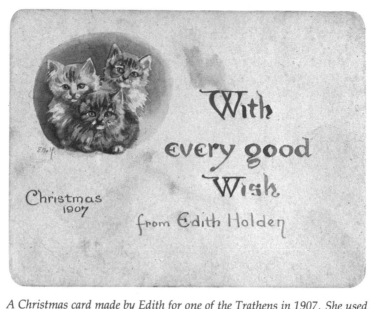

A Christmas card made by Edith for one of the Trathens in 1907. She used to write or paint one for each of the younger members of the family and continued to remember them at Christmas for many years.

A Christmas card made by Edith in 1909 for the Trathens.

An oil painting by Edith of Huckworthy Bridge on Dartmoor in the summer of 1908. She had visited the place with the Trathen girls and as it was a favourite spot of Bella's Edith gave her the painting as a wedding present.

The frontispiece from Animals Around Us, *illustrated by Edith.*

Sheep on Dartmoor, near Sheepstor, painted by Edith,
sent as a Christmas card to the Trathens.

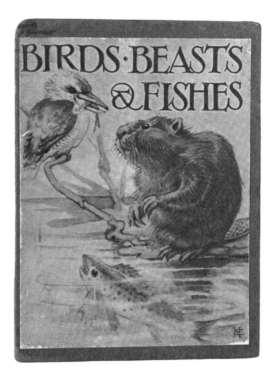

*The cover, frontispiece and an illustration
from* Birds, Beasts and Fishes. *The book
was illustrated entirely by Edith, and
was very small, obviously designed
for a child's hand.*

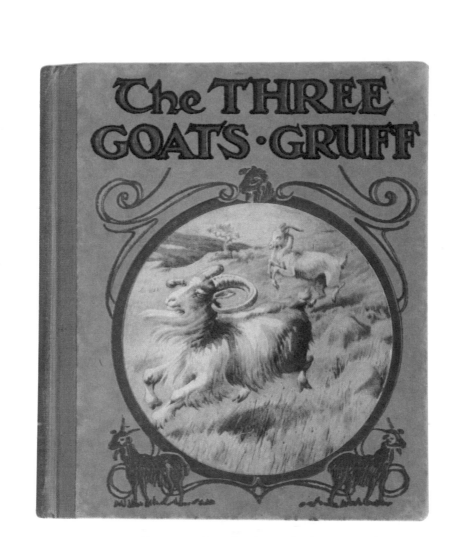

*The cover and two illustrations by Edith
for* The Three Goats Gruff.

A gold and opal ring which belonged to Edith.
It is thought to have been her engagement ring.
Opal was her birthstone.

Although she was unable to go to Dartmoor that year she did complete a painting of the area. On a previous visit she had begun a painting of Huckworthy Bridge which she had visited with Bella and Berta. Since it was a particular favourite with Bella, Edith promised to complete the oil painting as a wedding present for Bella and Robert Baker in August 1908.

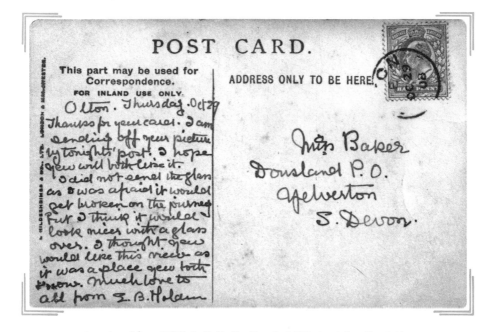

A postcard from Edith to Bella Trathen in 1908 about the oil painting of Huckworthy Bridge which was to be Bella's wedding present.

TEWKESBURY FROM THE MEADOWS.

COPYRIGHT.   E. J. BURROW

We went to this place last month with the mission party. It was a picnic.

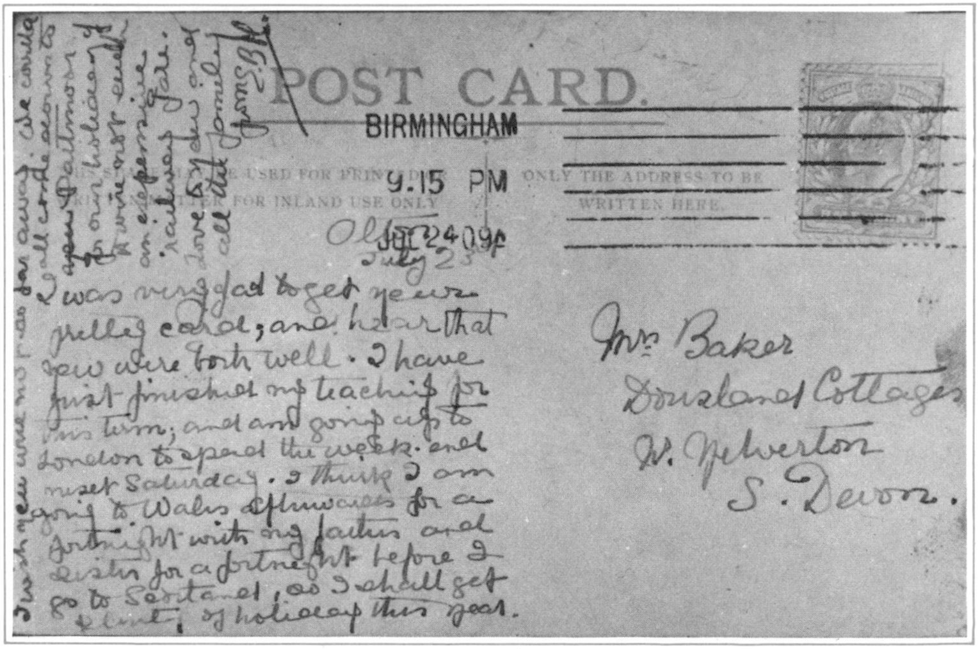

POST CARD.

BIRMINGHAM

9.15 PM

MAY BE USED FOR PRINTING
FOR INLAND USE ONLY

ONLY THE ADDRESS TO BE
WRITTEN HERE

I was very glad to get your jolly card, and hear that you were both well. I have just finished my teaching for this term, and am going up to London to spend the week-end next Saturday. I think I am going to Wales afterwards for a fortnight with my father and sister for a fortnight before I go to Scotland, so I shall get plenty of holiday this year.

Mrs Baker
Dousland Cottages
W. Yelverton
S. Devon.

Over the next few years the situation at home grew difficult for all members of the family. There had been grave financial problems in the Holden Company. Edith wrote to her friends at Dousland, "I wish you were not so far away. We could all come down to Dartmoor, if it were not such an expensive railway fare."

Edith did manage, however, to take her annual holiday in Scotland at Mrs Denovan Adam's boarding house but she now only went for two weeks.

She continued teaching but in the summer of 1909 went to London for several weeks and on one occasion wrote (in French) to Ernest Trathen:

Aug 21st 1909

My dear Pupil

There are lots of French people here this summer; they are here for the big exhibition. I was there last week, it was magnificent, above all, to see it when it is all lit-up. I have seen a lot of things in London, but my holiday is over next Monday. My kind regards to all the family. I hope that all is well.

Your friend
E. B. Holden

OPPOSITE
A card from Edith to Bella in July 1909 after Bella's marriage
just before Edith starts her summer holidays. She says she
is not able to go down to Dartmoor that year because the
train fare is too expensive. The card shows Tewkesbury in
Gloucestershire "from the meadows", where, Edith says, the
Holden annual works picnic had been held that year.

A drawing by Edith done in about 1908 taken from a scrapbook.
It is an embroidery design.

ABOVE AND OVERLEAF
Some examples of Edith's illustrations for
The Animals' Friend,
the magazine of the National Council for Animals' Welfare,
to which she contributed from 1907–10.

Edith mentioned nothing of her growing friendship with Ernest Smith, the young sculptor. She was then thirty-eight years old and accepted by her family as a spinster who would stay at home with her invalid sister Winifred, and together with Violet would look after their ageing father. Following the break up of Kenneth's marriage Edith's young nephew had arrived at Gowan Bank to be looked after. Edith was needed at home to help run the house especially as their diminished finances had led to a reduction in staff.

Ernest was a pupil of the eminent sculptor Professor Lanteri and had then graduated to being a pupil-teacher at the Royal College. He was, however, seven years Edith's junior and not the sort of match that Arthur Holden would have chosen for his daughter. Professor Lanteri held Ernest's work in high regard and acknowledged him in his famous book, *Modelling: a guide for Teachers and Students.*

Edith was fortunate in gaining various commissions for book illustrations on her trips to London and this gave her great hope for the future. She illustrated a children's story about a robin and a tortoise in a little book called *Daily Bread.*

In the preface to the book the publishers stated that they hoped it would be "a suitable gift at Christmas time" and that "the booklet may prove useful at gatherings for the encouragement of kindness to animals".

Edith was becoming established as an illustrator specializing in animals, so it was not surprising when she was approached to draw lions and polar bears to illustrate an article in *Mrs Strang's Annual For Children.* She was also commissioned to illustrate a collection of poetry for children called *Woodland Whisperings* and a natural history book for children called *Animals Around Us.*

ABOVE AND OVERLEAF
Some of Edith's illustrations for Daily Bread,
a children's story about a robin and a tortoise,
written by Margaret Gatty and published in 1910 when Edith
was thirty-nine. She sent a copy of the book to Bella
as a Christmas present.

ABOVE AND OPPOSITE
Some of the illustrations by Edith for Mrs Strang's Annual
for Children *for 1914 and c. 1925. The annual was a compilation*
of the work of various authors and illustrators, published every
year and it consisted of informative articles and drawings of animals.

A LITTLE TALK ABOUT GARDEN BIRDS

Baby Sparrows

ABOVE, OPPOSITE AND OVERLEAF
Illustrations by Edith for Animals Around Us
by Martin Merrythought, published in 1912.

THE HARE

THE WATER SHREW

THE SQUIRREL

THE HEDGEHOG

THE LONG-TAILED FIELD MOUSE

Edith Blackwell Holden married Alfred Ernest Smith on
1st June 1911 by special licence at Chelsea Register Office,
and they moved to a flat in Chelsea behind Cheyne Walk.
    Edith continued her illustrating work after her mar-
riage. Ernest was fortunate in gaining a new position in

his work. While at the Royal College of Art, he had been noticed by a distinguished sculptress, the Countess Feodora Gleichen, who took over her father's studio in St James's Palace.

The Countess invited Ernest to work for her as her principal assistant, which he accepted. He was required to reproduce in plaster the figure which the Countess modelled, and which she then worked on. When she had done that, Ernest would cast the figure in bronze. This was a skilled job and required someone who was a competent sculptor. The Countess had a great respect for Ernest's work and the partnership was most successful.

The studio at St James's Palace was a stimulating place to work in, and there were constant visitors from all walks of life. Members of visiting royalty came, like King Feisal when his bust was being sculpted, and leading members of the art and sculpture world. Sir George Frampton, who had recently gained fame for his statue of Peter Pan in Kensington Gardens, was a great friend of the Countess and a regular visitor.

Edith was always welcomed at the studio and found it fascinating, but she still followed her own career of book illustrating, and exhibited again at the Royal Academy in 1917.

CERTIFIED COPY OF AN ENTRY OF BIRTH

GIVEN AT THE GENERAL

Application F

	REGISTRATION DISTRICT *Kings Norton*						
1871.	BIRTH in the Sub-district of *Kings Norton*			in the *County of Wa*			

Columns:— 1	2	3	4	5	6	7	8
No.	When and where born	Name, if any	Sex	Name and surname of father	Name, surname and maiden surname of mother	Occupation of father	Signature, description and residence of informant	When registered
68	Twenty eighth September 1871 Church Road Kings Norton	Edith Blackwell	Girl	Arthur Holden	Emma Holden formerly Wearing	Manufacturer	Emma Holden Mother Church Road Kings Norton	Thirty first October 1871

CERTIFIED to be a true copy of an entry in the certified copy of a Register of Births in the District above mentioned.
Given at the GENERAL REGISTER OFFICE, LONDON, under the Seal of the said Office, the *8d* day of *November* 19

This certificate is issued in pursuance of the Births and Deaths Registration Act 1953. Section 34 provides that any certified copy of sealed or stamped with the seal of the General Register Office shall be received as evidence of the birth or death to which it relates wit proof of the entry, and no certified copy purporting to have been given in the said Office shall be of any force or effect unless it is sealed

BXA 251398

CAUTION:—Any person who (1) falsifies any of the particulars on this certificate, or (2) uses a falsified certificate as true, knowin to prosecution.

Form A502M (S.355267) Dd.323476 110M 12/75 H/w.

CERTIFIED COPY OF AN ENTRY OF MARRIAGE

Given at the GENERAL

Applie

	Registration District *Chelsea*					
1911.	Marriage solemnized at *the Register Office*					
in the *District* of *Chelsea*			in the *County of London*			

No.	When married	Name and Surname	Age	Condition	Rank or profession	Residence at the time of marriage
122	First June 1911.	Alfred Ernest Smith	32 years	Bachelor	Sculptor	4 Toubert Studios Jubilee Place Chelsea.
		Edith Blackwell Holden	39 years	Spinster	Artist (Painter)	Goryan Bank Kiveton Roga Olton Birmingham

Married in the *Register Office* according to the _____ of the_____ by

This marriage was solemnized between us, { *Ernest Smith* *Edith B. Holden* } in the presence of us, { *S. J. Hinton.* *E. A. Laurence* } IX Chas:

CERTIFIED to be a true copy of an entry in the certified copy of a Register of Marriages in the District above mentioned.
Given at the GENERAL REGISTER OFFICE, LONDON, under the Seal of the said Office, the *23ᵈ* day of *Nove*

This certificate is issued in pursuance of section 65 of the Marriage Act 1949. Sub-section (3) of that section provides that any certified cop be sealed or stamped with the seal of the General Register Office shall be received as evidence of the marriage to which it relates without any further and no certified copy purporting to have been given in the said Office shall be of any force or effect unless it is sealed or stamped as aforesaid.

MB 109116

CAUTION:—Any person who (1) falsifies any of the particulars on this certificate, or (2) uses a falsified certificate as true knowing it to be false, is liable to

A copy of Edith's birth certificate.

A copy of Edith's
marriage certificate.

*A photograph taken in 1912. Ernest Smith is standing in the
third row back, on the left, with his arm round the shoulder
of the person in front, and Frederick Smith is second
from the left in the row behind him. Professor Lanteri is
standing fourth from the left
in the front.*

OPPOSITE
*The Countess Feodora Gleichen (1861–1922) in her studio.
Her work can be found in many parts of the world
and when she died a fund was set up in her
name to give grants to women sculptors.*

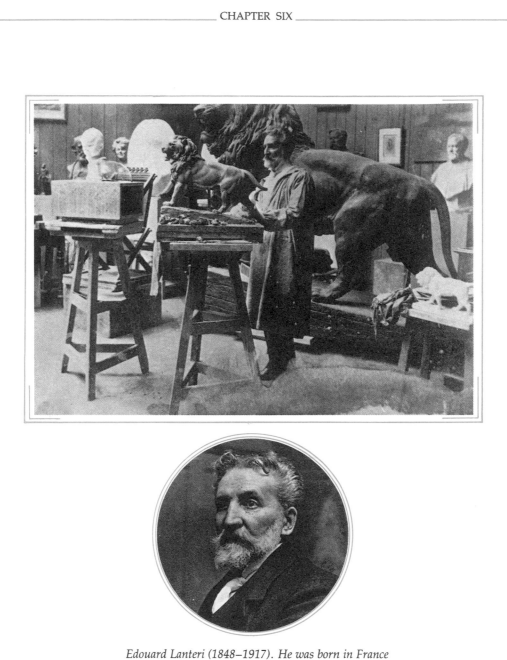

*Edouard Lanteri (1848–1917). He was born in France
and later became professor of sculpture at the
Royal College of Art, South Kensington, London.*

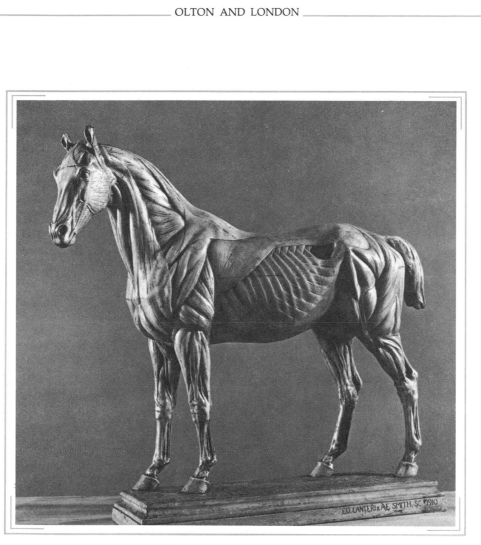

A statue which Lanteri and Ernest worked on together.
It is dated 1910 and both their names are on it.

*A photograph of Dorothy, Frederick Smith's wife,
taken before she was married
at the age of twenty-six.*

OPPOSITE
*A photograph taken in 1912 of Edith's brother-in-law,
Frederick Smith, an artist and craftsman.*

She also worked hard promoting the work of Ernest's brother Frederick, who was an artist and craftsman teaching at Wolverhampton School of Art. A sale of handwork was held at Chelsea Old Town Hall and Edith offered to man his stall of leatherwork. This letter to him gives an idea of her activity:

2 Oakley Cres.,
Chelsea, S.W. 3

Sunday Nov. 23rd 1919

Dear Fred,

After writing you yesterday I sold the blue card case (17/6) to Mad'elle De'lysia, — the actress who came in after her matinee just before closing time.

I tried to persuade her to have one of the white bags but she told me in her pretty broken English, that she did not like them, — no-one seemed at all tempted to buy them, — they thought them pretty but too delicate to be of use. Ernest arrived just before 6 p.m. and had a look round, — but many of the stall holders had packed up their goods by that time. Aunty M. also arrived, — so I had plenty of helpers to carry home the goods. I found your letter and other bag here when we got in. It is a pity you did not write to the 'Advert lady' direct, as I fear it will be too late now, I have written her today, — I hope it will reach her, I know neither her name nor address but have sent it under cover of the sec.ry of the Exhib. I am sending you a list of the sold and unsold things; I took £9.11.6 which I hope will

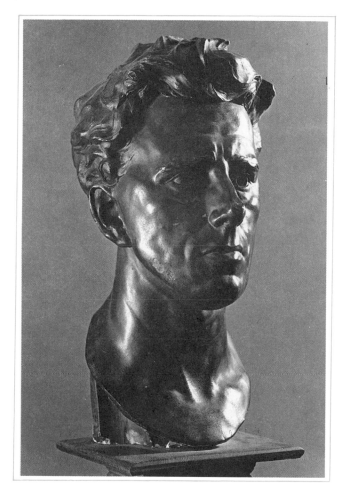

A bust of Frederick Smith by the sculptor Emerson
dated 1914.

clear your expenses though I don't suppose it will pay for the leather! — then there is the brush ordered — another 15/- and I hope you will receive some orders for the prayer books besides the order for the gentleman's note case. I have given away all your large cards. I will send you a cheque for the money I have taken within a few days, shall I deduct amount for insurance 3/4? — am waiting for a cheque to be sent me by Miss Harrison — must see whether she has made it out to you or me. A gentleman came round yesterday who said you would get any amount of book covers to do if you were to send specimens of your work to

Messrs. Sangoraki
Book binders
Carnaby Street

I wish I had been able to sell more for you — but it has been a splendid advertisement of your work which was admired by everyone. Ernest joins me in love to you, all 3.
Yours affectionately
Edith

There is little known about the nine years of Edith's married life until her death on Tuesday, 16th March 1920, when she was found drowned in a backwater of the Thames, near Kew Gardens Walk.

On the Monday morning she had complained to Ernest of a headache, but this was not uncommon and the matter had not been dwelt on. The main subject at breakfast had been the impending visit of some friends for Easter, to which Edith was looking forward. Ernest left for the studio at St James's Palace and Edith said that she would probably go down to the river later to see the University crews practising.

When Ernest returned home that evening his wife was out but the table had been laid for the evening meal, and Ernest assumed that she was with friends. It was not until the next morning that he learned the truth. Her body had been found at six o'clock on the Tuesday morning.

> '*The time of the singing of birds is come.*'—SONG OF SOLOMON.

In Loving Memory

of

EDITH BLACKWELL SMITH

(née Holden)

who passed into the fuller life of the Spirit, in her 49th year,
MARCH 15TH, 1920.

'For I reckon that the sufferings of this present time are not worthy to be compared with the glory that shall be revealed in us.'—ROMANS viii. 18.

"Our times are in His hand
Who saith 'A whole I planned,
Youth shows but half; trust God: see all
nor be afraid' "—BROWNING.

'Strew bay-leaves too, for God
To pass along.'   —A.K.M.

The In Memoriam *of Edith.*
The verses were chosen by Effie.

The inquest established that she had tried to reach a branch of chestnut buds. The bough was out of reach and with the aid of her umbrella Edith had tried to break it off, fallen forward into the river and drowned.

The family was stunned by her death. After her marriage, contact had not been close but nevertheless all felt this tragic loss. Some of the sisters who had been most distant from Edith wondered if her death might have been suicide, but those close to her knew it could not have been. Frederick's wife Dorothy had often discussed with Edith her spiritualist and religious views, and remembered how strongly Edith condemned suicide.

Drowned in the Ha-Ha.

AN ARTIST'S END.

The accidental death of Mrs. Edith Smith, of Oakley-crescent, Chelsea, was investigated by Dr. M. H. Taylor at the Richmond Coroner's Court on Thursday afternoon.

Alfred Smith identified the body of that of his wife, aged 47. He last saw her at 8.15 on Monday morning. On returning home he found the table laid, and he thought she had gone to see some friends. She had complained in the morning from headache, and witness advised her to go for a walk, and she replied that she would go Putney way. His wife had no trouble so far as he knew. She did some painting, and in order to get materials for her work she collected twigs.

Police-constable Cattle said that as he was walking down by the waterside on Tuesday morning, near Kew Gardens wall, he saw a woman lying face downwards in four feet of water in the Ha-Ha. In her hand was a bunch of twigs. It appeared as if she had been pulling down the branch of the tree with her umbrella, when she fell into the water. He sent for the police surgeon, who found life extinct.

Dr. Paine stated that death was due to drowning. There were no marks of violence or bruises or injuries on the body.

A verdict in accordance with the medical evidence was registered.

The body was cremated yesterday at Golders Green, Messrs. T. H. Sanders and Sons having charge of the arrangements.

An account of Edith's death in
The Richmond and Twickenham Times *for 20 March 1920.*

OPPOSITE
Edith's death as recorded in the Daily Sketch *for 17 March 1920.*

DAILY SKETCH, WEDNESDAY, MARCH 17, 1920.

LIGHT BLUES' HARD LUCK.

While Cambridge were attempting their first trial over the full course the boat became waterlogged, and they sprinted home.—(Daily Sketch.)

RIVER TRAGEDY. —Edith Smith (47), who was drowned in the Thames at Kew yesterday, is believed to have fallen in the water while gathering buds from chestnut trees.

SERVICE IN IRISH. — The Rev. T. Roche, who conducted a celebration of St. Patrick's Day at Holy Trinity, Dockhead, Bermondsey, in which the Irish language was used. —(Daily Sketch.)

B 574329

The Statutory Fee for this Certificate
is 3s. 7d., i.e., 2s. 7d. for the Certificate and
1s. for the Search if the Certificate is not
taken at the time of registration.

CERTIFIED COPY of an
Pursuant to the Births and Deaths

(S.O. 1543) Wt. 16119/148. 13,000 Bks. 8/18.—McC. & Co., Ltd., Ldn.—

Registration District. *Richmond*

1920 Death in the Sub-district of *Richm*

Columns :—	1	2	3	4	5
No.	When and where Died.	Name and Surname.	Sex.	Age.	Rank or Profession.
399	Found Dead 16 March 1920 The River Thames Kew n.d.	Edith Blackwell Smith	Female	48 years	Wife of Alfred Ernest Smith Sculptor 2 Oakley Crescent Chelsea

I, *Charles Lewis Fenn* Registrar of Births and Deaths for the Sub-dist
do hereby certify that this is a true copy of the Entry No. *399* in the Register Book of I

WITNESS MY HAND this *6th* day of *April* , 19 *20* .

*Edith's death certificate, establishing drowning
as the cause of her death.*

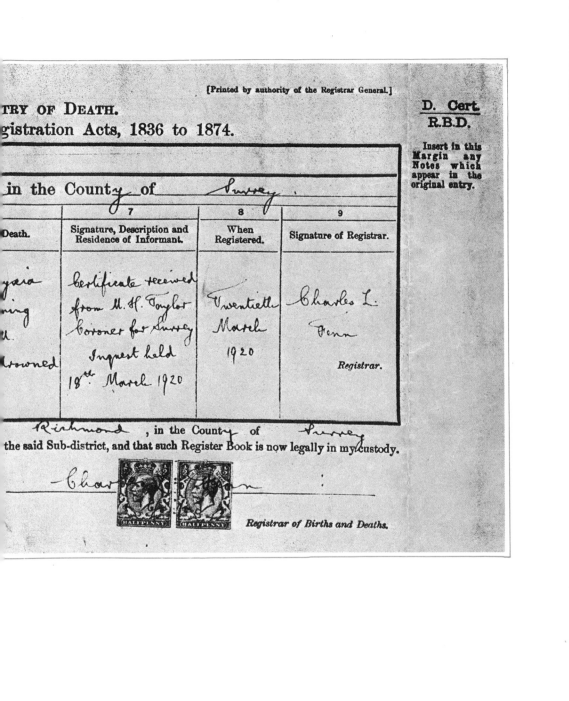

[Printed by authority of the Registrar General.]

...TRY OF DEATH.

...gistration Acts, 1836 to 1874.

D. Cert.
R.B.D.

Insert in this Margin any Notes which appear in the original entry.

...in the County of   *Surrey* .

...Death.	7 Signature, Description and Residence of Informant.	8 When Registered.	9 Signature of Registrar.
...gsia ...ning ...u. ...rowned	certificate received from M. H. Taylor Coroner for Surrey Inquest held 18th March 1920	Twentieth March 1920	Charles L. Fenn _Registrar._

Richmond , in the County of   *Surrey* the said Sub-district, and that such Register Book is now legally in my custody.

— Cha...

Registrar of Births and Deaths.

The Inquest into Edith Holden's death,
as reported in The West London Press, 19 March 1920

FOUND DROWNED
OAKLEY CRESCENT RESIDENT'S
STRANGE DEATH

THE TRAGIC CIRCUMSTANCES SURROUNDING the death of Edith Blackburn [*sic*] Smith aged 48 years of 2, Oakley Crescent, Chelsea, were described to Dr M. Taylor, the Richmond Coroner, who conducted an enquiry at the Richmond Coroner's Court yesterday (Thursday) afternoon.

Evidence of identification was given by Alfred Ernest Smith, sculptor, who stated that the deceased, his wife, was a painter. The last time he saw her alive was on Monday morning when she complained of a headache.

The Coroner: Did you leave home to go to work?
Witness: Yes.
Coroner: When you returned home what did you find? – My wife was not in, but the table was laid for the evening meal.
Was she in the habit of staying out in the evening? – No.
What did you think? – I thought she had either gone to see some friends or that she had gone to the theatre.
She was subject to neuralgia, I believe? – Yes.
Did she often come to Kew or the district? – She said that she would go by the river, and that she might see the University crews practising.
Did she know the river well? – Yes she knew this district (Richmond) well.
Have you ever known her to suffer from fainting attacks? – She would come over dizzy sometimes especially when she had a headache.
Was she in the habit of bringing home buds and flowers for the purpose of study? – Yes.
When did you think that something was wrong? – On Tuesday morning I went to the studio thinking that there might be a message as she didn't turn up on Monday night. When I returned I met a police constable who told me what had happened.
She was in the habit of going to Kew? – Yes, and Richmond Park.
Did she seem as usual on Monday morning? – Yes, quite, she was talking about some friends coming on a visit at Easter.
She was looking forward to that occasion? – Yes.

P.C. Cattell 1001V, said he was on duty near Kew Gardens Walk, about 6 o'clock on Tuesday morning, when he saw the body of a woman lying face downwards in the backwater of the Thames. He recovered the body and summoned the Divisional Surgeon of Police, who pronounced life extinct. Witness added that he found a small bunch of chestnut buds (produced) by the waterside and an examination revealed that one of the twigs had snapped off a bough of a tree which overhung the water. The bough was out of reach and, in order to secure it, the deceased had apparently stood on two stumps of wood with the idea of pulling it down with the aid of an umbrella which was found close to the body.

The Coroner: How deep is the water there?
Witness: About four or five feet.
If she lost her balance would she fall face downwards? – Yes she probably would.
And not backwards? – No I don't think so.
It is rather quiet round there, is it not? – Yes very quiet.
The likelihood is that if she met with an accident and shouted no-one would hear her?

Mr. Smith, recalled, said the deceased was a cool and collected woman who was not easily upset.
Dr. E. Payne, Divisional Surgeon of Police of Brunswick House, Kew, who made a post mortem examination of the body, said the deceased had apparently been in the water between 12 and 18 hours. The body was well-nourished and there were no external marks of injury. The lungs contained water and death was due to asphyxia, by drowning.

The Coroner: Do you know the spot where this happened?
Witness: Yes.
Do you think it possible that if she shouted it would not have been heard? – It is quite possible, there probably would not be anyone around there.

The Coroner recorded a verdict of "Found Drowned", the evidence being sufficient to definitely account for the manner in which the deceased got into the water.

The jacket of
The Country Diary of an Edwardian Lady,
first published in 1977,
nearly sixty years after
Edith's death.

Edith Holden

Ernest was completely heart-broken by the loss. He tried to carry on with his work after Edith's death but much of his strength seemed gone. Within eighteen months the Countess also had died and the world he knew seemed to be disintegrating. He left the flat in Chelsea and returned to the Joubert studios he had inhabited before his marriage, but he became ill and unable to work for a long time. He died in 1938.

THE COUNTRY DIARY OF AN EDWARDIAN LADY

Edith Holden

Michael Joseph
Webb & Bower

Edith Holden

Willow Warbler
feeding young.

In conversation Edith and Dorothy had discussed spiritualism and the possibility of life after death and perhaps with the publishing of her work Edith has come back, not as she anticipated, but in a way which has given pleasure to a greater number of people.

THE END

Paintings exhibited by Edith B. Holden
at the Royal Birmingham Society of Artists

The compiler is aware that some areas of Edith Holden's life still remain a mystery, and information would be welcomed from anyone whose family has memories of Edith. Of the fifty or so oil paintings which Edith exhibited none have so far come to light, but their titles are listed below.

1890 *A Cosy Quartette*
1891 *Springtime*
1892 *Rabbits*
    In the Time of Wild Roses
1893 *Amongst the Broom*
    A Friendly Visit
1894 *Head of St Bernard*
    Poultry
    Flowery Meadows
    Noontide
    Beside the Forth
1895 *Springtime: near Stirling*
    Poppies
    In Glen Dochart
1896 *On a Perthshire Moor*
    A Highland Refuge
    Playmates
    In the Valley of the Teith:
    Perthshire
1897 *On a Moorland Road:*
    Callander, Perthshire
    March Morning: Stirling
    Perthshire Highlanders
    A Moorland Sketch: October
1898 *Ladies First:*
    a couple of pedigree
    Dandie Dinmont terriers
    Under the Greenwood Tree

1899 *In the Isle of Arran*
    The Guardian of the Raid
1900 *Rabbits*
    Changing Pasture: Perthshire
    Highland Calves
    Study of Highland Cattle
    Milking Time
1901 *Babes in the Wood*
    A Welsh Stream
    In the Perthshire Highlands
1902 *On a Surrey Farmstead*
    A Wintry Gleam: Dartmoor
1903 *On the Banks of the Firth*
    Study of Highland Cattle
    In the Golden Days
1904 *Friend or Foes?*
    Edmund Street, Birmingham:
    A November Day
    Hauling Timber
1905 *A Portrait*
    The Rowan Tree
1906 *Study of Chaffinch's Nest*
    and Hawthorns
    Study of Hedge-Sparrow's
    Nest
    Dartmoor Ponies
1907 *A Moorland Pasture*

Edith Holden exhibited *The Rowan Tree* at the Royal Academy of Arts in 1907 and, as Mrs Edith Smith, *Young Bears Playing* in 1917.

BIBLIOGRAPHY

The Animals' Friend, the magazine of the National Council for Animals' Welfare, vols 13–16 1907–10 with illustrations by Edith Holden (GEORGE BELL & SONS)

Daily Bread, Margaret Gatty, illustrated by Edith Holden (GEORGE BELL & SONS, 1910)

Woodland Whisperings, Margaret Rankin, illustrated by Edith Holden (GEORGE BELL & SONS, 1911)

Animals Around Us, Martin Merrythought, illustrated by Edith Holden (HUMPHREY MILFORD/OXFORD UNIVERSITY PRESS, 1912)

Birds, Beasts and Fishes, various authors, illustrated by Edith Holden (HENRY FROWDE/HODDER & STOUGHTON, date unknown)

The Three Goats Gruff, Helen van Cleve Blankmeyer, illustrated by Edith Holden (HENRY FROWDE/HODDER & STOUGHTON, date unknown)

Mrs Strang's Annual for Children, various authors, some illustrations by Edith Holden (HENRY FROWDE/HODDER & STOUGHTON)

The Hedgehog Feast, Rowena Stott, illustrated by Edith Holden (MICHAEL JOSEPH/WEBB & BOWER, 1978)

The Country Diary of an Edwardian Lady, Edith Holden,

UK and Commonwealth	MICHAEL JOSEPH/WEBB & BOWER, 1977
USA	HOLT, RINEHART & WINSTON, 1977
Sweden	TREVI, 1978
Germany	FRIEDRICH W. HEYE, 1979
Finland	OTAVA, 1979
Norway	J. W. CAPPELENS, 1979
Denmark	LINDHARDT OG RINGHOF, 1979
Holland	ZOMER & KEUNING BOEKEN, 1979
Italy	ARNOLDO MONDADORI EDITORE, 1979
Spain	EDITORIAL BLUME, 1979
Japan	SANRIO, 1980
France	EDITIONS BLUME/DU CHÊNE, 1980

Beatrice of St. Mawse, Emma Wearing (MORGAN, 1864)

Ursula's Girlhood, Emma Wearing (SOCIETY FOR PROMOTING CHRISTIAN KNOWLEDGE, 1867)

A Book of Pictured Carols, ed. A. J. Gaskin, one illustration by Violet Holden (GEORGE ALLEN, 1893)

The Real Princess, Blanche Atkinson, illustrated by Violet and Evelyn Holden (INNES, 1894)

The House that Jack Built, illustrated by Violet and Evelyn Holden (DENT & CO., 1895)

The Yellow Book vol. 9, one illustration by Evelyn Holden (1896)

Art, Paint and Vanity, Arthur Ll. Matthison (HEATH CRANTON LTD, 1934)

ACKNOWLEDGEMENTS

The compiler would like to acknowledge the following for their help during the preparation of this book:

Miss Rowena Stott, the great-niece by marriage of Edith Holden; Mrs Irene Abbott; the Archives of the Art and Design Centre of Birmingham Polytechnic College; Mrs Kathleen Ashford; Mr Leslie Brannan; the Bristol Library; the British Library; Mr Graeme Chapman; the Chelsea Library; Mr Alan Crawford; Ms Lynda Davis; the Glasgow Library; the Glasgow Museum and Art Gallery; Mr Hector Goldsack; the Guildford Library; Ms Celia Haddon; Miss Doris Hamilton-Smith; Mrs Dorothy Hope; Mrs Lilian Horn; Mr and Mrs Eric Hotchkiss; Mr Terry Jones; Mr Roger Machell; Miss Kaila Matthison; Miss Doris Meyer; National Gallery of Scotland; Mr Carol Palmer; Mr Kenneth Palmer; Mrs Vyvyan Palmer; Mr Wilbert Palmer; Mrs Sheila Pearsall; the Plymouth Library; Mrs Hilda Rees; the Royal Academy; the Royal Archives; the Royal Scottish Academy; the Royal Society for the Prevention of Cruelty to Animals; Mrs Mary Sandbach; the Sandeman Library, Perth; the Society of Friends; the Society for Promoting Christian Knowledge; the Solihull Library; Mrs Celia Stevens; the Stirling Archives; the Stirling Library; the Stirling Smith Art Gallery; Mrs Freda Stott; Mr Philip Sturge; Mr Percy Trathen; the Warwickshire County Record Office; Ms Alison Wright; and especially her husband Colin.

The Publishers would like to thank the following for their kind permission to use material for illustration:

The Birmingham Reference Library, *pages 13, 17, 26, 27, 29, 30, 33, 34, 52, 53*; the British Library, *pages 165–7*; Mr Graeme Chapman, *page 117*; the Chelsea Library, *pages 196–7*; Miss Doris Hamilton-Smith, *pages 78, 79, 116, 123, 138*; Holden Surface Coatings Ltd, *pages 14, 22, 55, 92*; Mrs Dorothy Hope, *pages 132–5*; Mrs Lilian Horn, *pages 72, 99, 145*; Mr Eric Hotchkiss, *pages 112, 113*; Mr Roger Machell, *page 182*; Mr Archibald McLaren and the Stirling Archives, *pages 124, 125*; Miss Kaila Matthison, *pages 56, 57, 61*; the National Library of Scotland, *pages 46 and 47*; Mr W. Carol T. Palmer, *page 77*; Mr Kenneth C. T. Palmer, *pages 71, 96, 97, 146*; Mrs Vyvyan Palmer, *pages 73 (below), 108, 120, 136–7, 143, 144, 152, 153, 161, 162*; Mr Wilbert G. T. Palmer, *pages 102, 155*; Mrs Hilda Rees, *pages 15, 82, 84, 85, 86, 88, 89*; Mrs Celia Stevens, *pages 42, 43, 44, 49, 65, 66, 68, 69, 70, 91, 94*; Miss R. Rowena Stott, *pages 62, 63, 67, 68 (above), 74, 75, 76, 139, 140, 150, 154, 156, 157, 158, 159, 160, 164, 174–7, 183, 184, 185, 186, 187, 189, 191, 192, 193, 200*; Mr Percy Trathen, *page 77*; Mrs Anne C. Williams, *jacket front, frontispiece, pages 73 (above), 100, 101, 103, 104, 106, 109, 119, 132–5, 141, 151, 152, 169–71*.

Uncaptioned illustrations throughout the book have been taken from *The Animals' Friend* by kind permission of Mrs Dorothy Hope and Mrs Anne Williams, and from *Animals Around Us* and *Woodland Whisperings* by kind permission of Miss R. Rowena Stott.

The Publishers would also like to thank Mr Michael Alexander who took many of the photographs.

INDEX

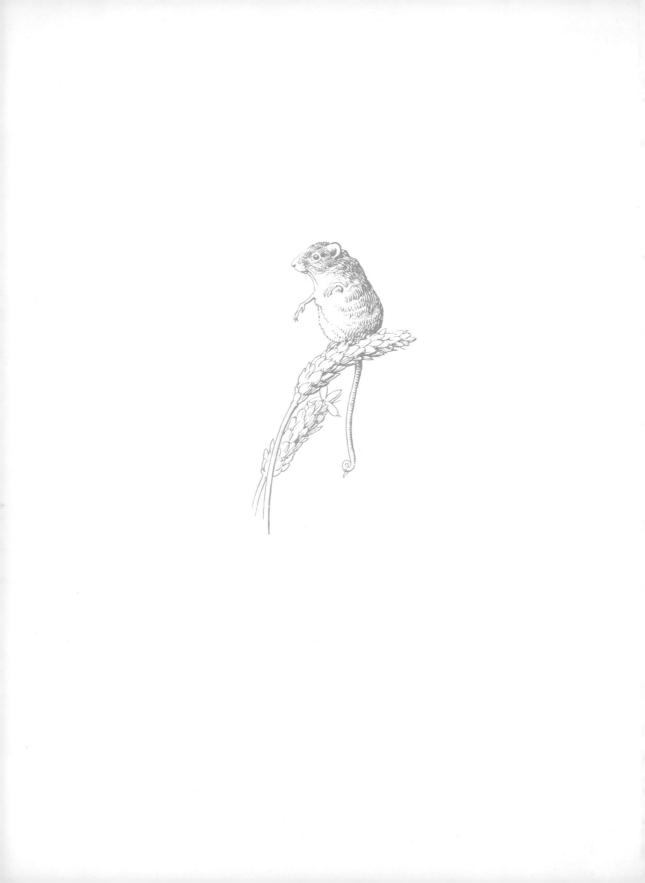

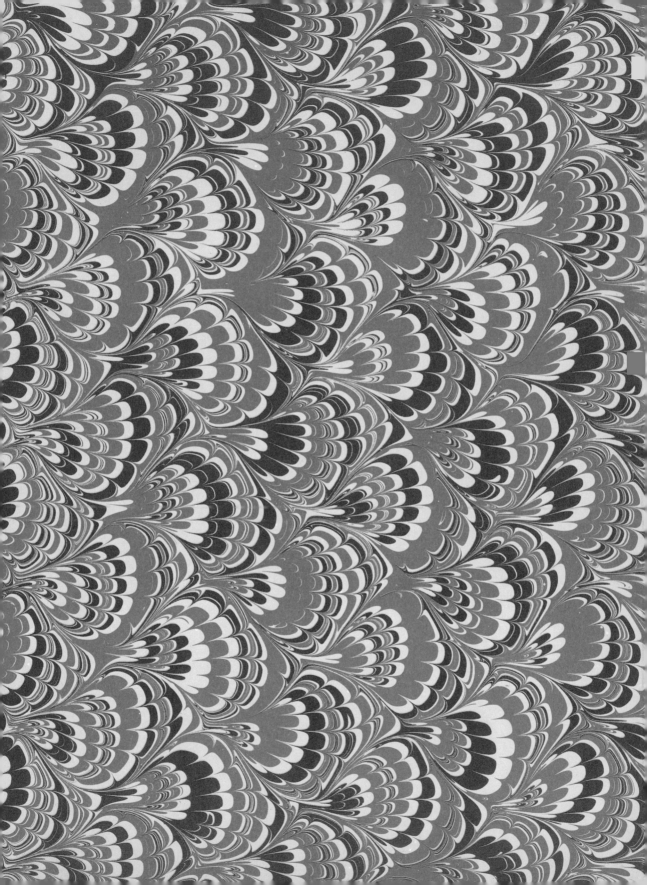